THE
FOUNDATIONS
OF
FAITH

VOLUME ONE

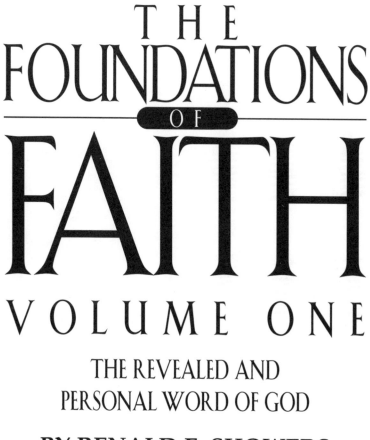

THE FOUNDATIONS OF FAITH

VOLUME ONE

THE REVEALED AND PERSONAL WORD OF GOD

BY RENALD E. SHOWERS

The Friends of Israel Gospel Ministry, Inc.
P.O. Box 908, Bellmawr, NJ 08099

THE FOUNDATIONS OF FAITH, VOLUME ONE
THE REVEALED AND PERSONAL WORD OF GOD

Renald E. Showers

Library of Congress Catalog Card Number: 2002103725
ISBN 0–915540–77–0

Cover design by Design Pointe, Salem, OR.

Visit our Web site at *www.foi.org*.

TABLE OF CONTENTS

DEDICATION

This book is dedicated with great respect and appreciation to Fred Raupp and Paul Golden, my sons-in-law and fellow servants in the ministry.

INTRODUCTION

This book begins the first in a set of volumes presenting the doctrines contained in the Bible—doctrines that constitute the foundations of the Christian faith. The word *doctrine* comes from the Latin term *doctrina*, which means "instruction, education, learning."[1] It also refers to "that which is taught; what is held, put forth as true."[2] Thus biblical doctrine consists of those divine truths that are recorded in the Scriptures and intended by God to be taught. The apostle Paul wrote, "All scripture is given by inspiration of God, and is profitable for doctrine [lit., teaching]" (2 Tim. 3:16).

Divisions of Biblical Doctrine

Over centuries of diligent study, Bible students have discovered that Scripture's divine truths fall into several categories or divisions of doctrine. The names assigned to those divisions and their meanings are as follows:

> *Bibliology*—the study of the Bible
> *Theology Proper*—the study of God
> *Angelology*—the study of angels, including *Satanology*—the study
>   of Satan and *Demonology*—the study of demons
> *Anthropology*—the study of man
> *Hamartiology*—the study of sin
> *Christology*—the study of Christ
> *Soteriology*—the study of salvation
> *Pneumatology*—the study of the Spirit
> *Ecclesiology*—the study of the church
> *Eschatology*—the study of last things

Negative Attitude Toward Doctrine

Tragically, many Christians have a negative attitude toward doctrine. They express this negativity in various ways. Some claim that doctrine divides people; therefore, it should not be taught. Apparently they do not recognize the serious implication of that claim. Since biblical doctrine consists of those divine truths recorded in Scripture, these people essentially are saying that God's truth divides; therefore, His truth should not be taught.

If division occurs when correct doctrine is taught, it is not the fault of doctrine or the teaching of doctrine. Instead, it is because people react wrongly to the doctrine. They refuse to accept biblical truth and its implications, so they separate themselves from those who do accept and teach it.

Others say, "Doctrine is not important. What is important is experience." Several years ago, when a pastor visited a couple from his church who were beginning to move in a dangerous direction, the husband raised his hand to his chin and said, "Pastor, we're fed up to here with the Word of God. We don't want God's Word anymore. What we want is experience." Probably without realizing it, that man revealed he had been greatly influenced by the existentialist philosophy that so thoroughly permeates our society. An existentialist contends, "The only thing that is important is what is meaningful to me personally."

Is it true that doctrine is not important? God doesn't think so. Many years ago I read an article that so impressed me I have never forgotten its content. At the beginning of a seminary course on New Testament studies, an instructor told his students that they would work together on one major project that semester. They would move systematically through the New Testament to categorize every area of truth and determine how many times each area is addressed. Their goal was to find the one truth emphasized more than any other in the New Testament. When they completed the project, they were amazed to see that warning against false doctrine is emphasized more than any other issue—even more than love, unity, and experience.

Since God inspired the Scriptures, this discovery is significant. It indicates that doctrine is of paramount importance to God. Since it is so important to Him, it had better be important to His people.

Valid spiritual experience exists, and such experience is important; but to be valid, it must agree with God's truth. Many false spiritual experiences are available to people. In light of this situation, it is critical that God's people have an objective, authoritative standard by which to evaluate experiences and determine which are valid and which are false. That standard consists of the doctrinal truths of God's Word. Thus, in order to avoid the false, it is imperative that God's people know biblical doctrine. Those who do not are vulnerable and are like a ship without its anchor.

Still others assert, "Doctrine is not important. Love and unity are important." Indeed, proper love and unity *are* important; but, as we have seen, so is doctrine. The apostle John used the words *love* and *truth* many times in his Gospel and epistles, indicating that God's people are to hold onto both. Several times John tied love and truth together, implying that they are to be related to each other. Doctrine that is not united with love becomes dead orthodoxy, but love that is divorced from correct doctrine can be perverted or false. For this reason, John talked about loving people "in the truth" (2 Jn. 1; 3 Jn. 1).

Today there is a dangerous tendency to sacrifice and compromise God's truth for the sake of unity. For example, for the sake of unity with people who do not hold to the true gospel necessary for salvation, some have gone so far as to say that those people are to be regarded as true Christians; and no attempt should be made to evangelize them. This tendency stands in stark contrast with the examples of Christ, who refused to sacrifice God's truth for the sake of unity with the Pharisees and Sadducees (Mt. 16:5–12; 23), and Paul, who would not compromise the true gospel for the sake of unity with the Judaizers (Gal. 1:6–12).

The tragedy of love and unity being divorced from doctrinal truth is expressed graphically in a poem about two sisters (Love and Unity) who married two husbands (Doctrine and Truth):

A TALE OF TWO SISTERS
or The Tragedy of Ecumenical Unfaithfulness

With heart so kind and gentle,
And sympathetic eye;
With touching, deep affection,
And loyal, tender tie—
Was LOVE betrothed to DOCTRINE
To hold him all her days:
And walk the aisle of gladness
United in His ways.

Her younger sister also
Had qualities as fair,
Of caring, selfless, kindness,
And warmth without compare;
Thus UNITY was drawn to

The husband of her youth:
And pledged herself for ever
To be the bride of TRUTH.

But TIME, with bitter envy,
Across the testing years,
Pursued the slow erosion
Of happiness to tears;
Till LOVE began to weary
Of DOCTRINE'S pleasant voice,
And UNITY grew cold to
The partner of her choice.

Then LOVE began to notice
The charms of HERESY,
And awed by his opinions,
She wanted to be free;
And UNITY perceived that
Her virtues were desired
By many, many others
Whose ways she so admired.

At length, two precious unions,
So promising, so blest,
Were darkened by delusion,
Disloyalty, unrest;
Till came the day of sorrows,
And rending vows of youth,
When LOVE divorced her DOCTRINE,
And UNITY her TRUTH.
                              —Author unknown

Still others claim that the study of doctrine can cause a person to lose his or her zeal for the Lord and grow spiritually lukewarm or even cold. This assertion also has a serious implication. Since biblical doctrine consists of those divine truths that are recorded in the Scriptures, in essence they are saying that God's truth can cause loss of zeal for the Lord and a lukewarm or cold spiritual condition.

Some people do lose their zeal and grow lukewarm or cold while studying doctrine, but that is not the fault of biblical doctrine or the study of it. Instead, it is because of a person's wrong response to doctrine. He or she is not allowing God's truth to make its intended lifechanging impact.

Those Christians who make negative statements about doctrine and the teaching of doctrine thereby expose their spiritual deformity. The Scriptures assert that inability to receive in-depth teaching of God's truth is an indication of carnality and lack of spirituality (1 Cor. 3:1–3), as well as immaturity (Heb. 5:11–14).

Why would God reveal His doctrinal truths and have them recorded in inspired, permanent form in the Bible if He weren't vitally concerned that His people learn them?

Dangerous Trend

There is a discernible, growing trend to move away from the systematic teaching of doctrine in churches that claim to be Bible-believing. It is becoming increasingly more difficult to find a church that provides such instruction. This situation is so prevalent that a Bible conference awhile back conducted a forum called "Doctrine—The Endangered Species."

This trend stands in stark contrast to the practice of the early church. The believers of the first century "continued steadfastly in the apostles' doctrine" (Acts 2:42). The word translated "continued steadfastly" means "to occupy oneself diligently with something," "to pay persistent attention to," "to hold fast to something."[3] Thus the early Christians apparently occupied themselves diligently with, paid persistent attention to, or held fast to doctrine every time they gathered together. With this in mind, Walter Grundmann wrote:

> Luke sketches the Christian community for us in Acts 2:42. With assembly for prayer we find the common meal, fellowship and apostolic doctrine. Persistence in these things is a practical fulfillment of the direction of the Lord to "continue in my word" (Jn. 8:31). Hence the word proskarterein, used to describe the life of the community, expresses one aspect of the power and vitality of primitive Christianity.[4]

Paul issued the following command to Timothy: "And the things that thou hast heard from me among many witnesses, the same commit thou to faithful men, who shall be able to teach others also" (2 Tim. 2:2). The fact that this is a command indicates that each generation of Christians has a divinely imposed obligation to teach biblical doctrine to the next one. This command contains a frightening implication. If one generation fails to teach doctrine to the next one, that generation and every one thereafter will be ignorant of God's truth and vulnerable to every kind of error. The church will be severely harmed and will change radically into something that God never intended.

In light of this situation, the present trend of churches moving away from the systematic teaching of biblical doctrine is not only dangerous but has frightening implications for the spiritual welfare of individual believers and the church.

THE
REVEALED WORD
OF GOD

CHAPTER ONE

DIVINE
REVELATION

In the study of biblical doctrine, it is essential to begin with the doctrine of the Bible (bibliology), which consists of biblical teaching about itself. Since all other biblical doctrines are derived from the Bible, the doctrine of the Bible about itself is the foundation on which all other doctrines are based. If the Bible presents error concerning itself, then all the rest of biblical doctrine rests on a faulty foundation and is thereby subject to question.

The Bible professes to be the written record of truths revealed by God to mankind. In light of this claim, we'll begin the study of the doctrine of the Bible with an examination of the subject of divine revelation, starting with its definition.

DEFINITION OF DIVINE REVELATION

To establish a definition of divine revelation, we must first examine several facts.

Biblical Words for Revelation

The major Hebrew Old Testament verb related to revelation (*galah*) basically means "to uncover" as well as "to show, to reveal, to make known."[1]

The most significant Greek New Testament verb associated with revelation *(apocalupto)*[2] means "to uncover, reveal, disclose, bring to light."[3]

The meanings of both of these words indicate that revelation involves the uncovering of knowledge.

Difference Between Revelation and Discovery

There is a significant difference between revelation and discovery of knowledge. When discovery takes place, the receiver of knowledge is active. He is uncovering the knowledge by himself, rather than another person uncovering it for him. Thus discovery can involve only one person and a body of knowledge.

By contrast, when revelation occurs, the receiver of knowledge is passive. Someone else uncovers knowledge for him or her. Thus revelation always involves at least two people (the revealer and the receiver) and a body of knowledge. In the case of divine revelation, the revealer is God; and the receiver is human. In line with this, Albrecht Oepke, wrote, "In the strict sense revelation is always and everywhere the act of God. No one has a right to it simply because he is a man."[4]

Object of Revelation

The object of revelation is what is revealed. When revelation takes place, that which is revealed is a body of knowledge that formerly had been hidden from the receiver of knowledge. Thus Oepke indicated that revelation involves "the unveiling of what is hidden."[5]

When divine revelation occurs, the object of revelation is a body of knowledge that formerly had been hidden from mankind and that mankind could never discover on its own, no matter how much time is given to try every possible means. If God had not chosen to uncover that knowledge, mankind would be ignorant of it forever. This object of divine revelation is indicated in at least two New Testament passages.

1 Corinthians 2:6–10

In the first five verses of 1 Corinthians 2, Paul asserted that when he came to the Corinthians to minister, he did not present the philosophical wisdom of mankind to those Greeks who loved such wisdom. He purposely avoided giving his hearers what they desired because he wanted their faith to rest on the enduring foundation of God's power, not on the shaky wisdom of man, which is continually changing as one philosophical fad is exchanged for another.

Beginning with verse 6, Paul hastened to declare that although he did not present philosophical wisdom to the Corinthians, he did give them wisdom, not ignorance. But the wisdom he presented was not the naturalistic, man-centered wisdom characteristic of this age, nor was it the wisdom of authoritative officials who direct the affairs of the present world system. Their wisdom is short-lived because they are temporary.

The wisdom Paul spoke of was God's (v. 7). He declared that he spoke God's wisdom "in a mystery." In the New Testament, the word *mystery* means "the secret thoughts, plans, and dispensations of God which are hidden [from] the human reason, as well as [from] all other comprehension below the divine level, and hence must be revealed to those for whom they are intended."[6] Paul asserted that the divine wisdom he presented was in the form of a body of knowledge that had been hidden from man and that man could not discover through his natural resources.

Paul made this assertion clear by giving four additional descriptions of God's wisdom. First, it was "the hidden wisdom."

Second, it was "ordained" (literally, "foreordained") by God "before the ages." God had determined this body of knowledge before earth's history began, and thus He possessed this knowledge from eternity past. As a result, this wisdom had been hidden from man but not from God.

Third, all the authoritative officials who directed the affairs of the present world system were totally ignorant of this wisdom (v. 8). Paul gave the following proof of their ignorance: If they had known this wisdom of God, they would not have crucified Jesus Christ, "the Lord of glory." They would have recognized who He was and His significance.

Fourth, man cannot discover this divine wisdom through his natural resources (v. 9). On the basis of Isaiah 64:4, Paul indicated that the human senses, such as sight and hearing, are incapable of uncovering this knowledge. In addition, he asserted that human reason ("the heart of man") cannot perceive it. The Scriptures often regard the heart "as the organ of thinking."[7] For example, they speak of a man thinking in his heart (Prov. 23:7), people understanding with their hearts (Mt. 13:15), and evil thoughts proceeding out of man's heart (Mk. 7:21).

This teaching of Paul posed a potential problem. If mankind could not discover this wisdom through the use of the human senses and ability to reason, how did Paul obtain it? Was he some kind of supersaint? Did he possess extrasensory perception? He set the record straight by declaring that he obtained this divine body of knowledge by revelation from God (v. 10). He did not acquire it through some human resource he possessed.

Ephesians 3:3–11

Paul recorded significant truths concerning Jesus Christ. Apparently he anticipated that his readers would be so impressed with them that they would wonder how he obtained them. So they would understand the source of these truths, he declared that he had received them by revelation from God (vv. 3–4). Through the use of the terms *known* and *knowledge,* Paul signified that it was a body of knowledge that was revealed to him. Three times in Ephesians 3, Paul called this revealed body of knowledge "the mystery" (vv. 3–4, 9). In addition, he indicated a relationship between this body of knowledge and "the manifold wisdom of God" (v. 10).

Paul taught that this body of knowledge corresponded to God's eternal purpose (v. 11). Thus God possessed it through past ages of time, but it was hidden from mankind until God revealed it to His apostles and prophets in New Testament times (vv. 5, 9).

The specific content of this body of knowledge to which Paul referred in Ephesians 3 was not the fact that Gentiles would be saved. That fact was not hidden from mankind in the ages before New Testament times. All those who were saved before Abraham were Gentiles (e.g., Abel, Enoch, Noah and his wife), and a number of Israel's Old Testament prophets referred to Gentile salvation.

Instead, the content of "the mystery" in Ephesians 3 indicated that there would be a period of time during which Gentile believers of the gospel would be brought together as equals with Jewish believers to form one body, the church. They would be made joint heirs and joint partakers of God's promise in Christ with Jewish believers (vv. 6–10; cf. Eph. 2:11–22; Col. 1:25–27). In line with this truth, G. Bornkamm wrote, "In Eph. 3:4ff. the mystery is the share of the Gentiles in the inheritance, in the body of the Church, in the promise in Christ. This joining of Jews and Gentiles in one body under the head of Christ is a cosmic eschatological event."[8]

Through his treatment of the concept of *mystery* in 1 Corinthians 2 and Ephesians 3, Paul taught that the object of divine revelation is a body of knowledge that formerly had been hidden from mankind and that mankind could never discover on its own. For this reason Bornkamm stated,

The mystery is not itself revelation; it is the object of revelation . . . revelation discloses the mystery as such. Hence the mystery of God does not disclose itself. At the appointed time it is in free grace declared by God Himself to those who are selected and blessed by Him.[9]

Resultant Definition

On the basis of what we have observed concerning the biblical words for revelation, the difference between revelation and discovery, and the object of revelation, it is now possible to form a definition of divine revelation. Divine revelation is the uncovering by God for mankind of a body of knowledge formerly hidden from mankind and totally undiscoverable by mankind.

KINDS OF DIVINE REVELATION

Scripture indicates two kinds or categories of divine revelation. Theologians have assigned the following titles to them.

General Revelation

General revelation is God's uncovering of knowledge through means available to all mankind in general.

Special Revelation

Special revelation is God's uncovering of knowledge through special means not always available to all mankind in general.

CONCLUSION

God has revealed to mankind knowledge about Himself; the origin, purpose, responsibilities, and ultimate destiny of mankind; His plan and purpose for history; His provision of salvation from the penalty for our sins; and how we can obtain that salvation. The Bible is the written record of those divinely revealed truths. It is not the human account of an evolutionary development of spiritual consciousness by mankind. Therefore, it is imperative that mankind heed the biblical divine revelation.

CHAPTER TWO

GENERAL
REVELATION

There are two kinds or categories of divine revelation: general and special. General revelation is God's uncovering of knowledge through means available to all mankind. The Scriptures indicate that God uses three major means of general revelation: nature, history, and conscience. God can use these as means of general revelation because all people are exposed to nature and history, and every person has a conscience.

NATURE

At least three biblical passages indicate that God uncovers knowledge to man through nature.

Psalm 19:1–6

David began Psalm 19 by stating, "The heavens declare the glory of God, and the firmament showeth his handiwork" (v. 1).

The word translated "glory" (kabod) means "to be heavy, weighty."[1] The Bible uses it most frequently in a figurative sense for "the concept of a 'weighty' person in society, someone who is honorable, impressive, worthy of respect."[2] Thus a person's glory is anything concerning that person that causes him or her to carry weight with others. It is that which is impressive and demands recognition, gives a person influence, sets that person apart, and distinguishes him or her from others. For example, Jacob's great wealth and Joseph's powerful position as an official of Egypt are called their glory (Gen. 31:1, KJV; 45:13). These things gave these men influence and recognition and impressed others.

The word translated "showeth" means "to place a matter high, conspicuous before a person."[3]

In light of these meanings of *glory* and *showeth*, we can conclude that in Psalm 19:1 David said the heavens declare what is impressive or influential concerning God. They display what should be obvious to the human eye and mind—namely, the conspicuous, distinctive stamp of His divine handiwork. The magnitude, beauty, order, and design of the heavens testify to the existence, wisdom, and power of their Creator.

Have you been impressed with the existence and greatness of God while gazing at the magnificent star-studded heavens on a clear night? If not, perhaps some data concerning the universe will help to impress you. Are you aware that planet earth weighs approximately 6,600 quintillion tons (6,600 with an additional 18 zeros)?[4] To convert this astronomical figure into pounds, you must multiply it by 2,000.

The earth is huge in contrast to each human; but in comparison with the sun in our solar system, it is small. Did you know that 1.3 million earths are needed to match the volume of our sun?[5]

The sun is enormous, and yet it is one of the smallest stars in our galaxy. Another star, Antares, is so gigantic that it occupies 90 million times as much space as our sun and is 390 million miles in diameter.[6]

In spite of its great size, Antares is only one of approximately 100 billion stars in our galaxy.[7] Our galaxy is so massive that it takes 100,000 years for light, traveling at approximately 186,000 miles a second, to move from one end to the other.[8] It is so thick that 5,000 to 10,000 years are needed for light to travel from the top to the bottom.[9]

Although our galaxy is so vast, it is only one of approximately one billion galaxies that astronomers were able to photograph until a few years ago.[10] As new techniques and instruments for probing the heavens continue to be developed, even more galaxies are discovered. Recently "the world's largest optical telescope has captured an image of the most distant galaxy known. . . . The galaxy lies approximately 12 to 15 billion light-years from the Milky Way" and "spans 200,000 light-years in diameter."[11]

Are you beginning to feel a little insignificant? Why did God create a universe of such magnitude, beauty, order, and design? He did it to impress His human creatures with His existence and greatness so that He could have life-changing influence in their lives. As a result of observing the heavens, we should be impressed with God's infinity and our own finiteness. David expressed such an attitude: "When I consider thy heavens, the work of thy fingers, the moon and the stars, which thou hast ordained, What is man, that thou art mindful of him? And the son of man, that thou visitest him?" (Ps. 8:3–4).

In Psalm 19:2 David emphasized a time factor: "Day unto day uttereth speech, and night unto night showeth knowledge." While quoting from Keil and Delitzsch's *Commentary on the Old Testament*, Leonard J. Coppes stated the following significance for the verb translated "uttereth": "In Ps 19:2 *naba* images the 'uninterrupted line of transmission' and 'inexhaustible spring,' the 'day' issuing in declaring God's glory."[12] David indicated there is no time limit on this revelation of knowledge concerning God through the heavens. It has been going on 24 hours a day without interruption since the beginning of time. Thus, regardless of what time period a person has lived in on earth, he or she has been exposed to this revelation.

In verse 3 David emphasized a language factor: "No speech, no languages; their voice is not heard" (literal translation). There is no audible speech, no language involved in this revelation that comes through the heavens. It is a totally silent communication of knowledge concerning God. Because it does not come in the form of languages, there are no language barriers to its effective communication. As a result, people of all languages can understand this revelation.

In verse 4 David emphasized a geographical factor: "Their line is gone out through all the earth, and their words to the end of the world." According to Earl S. Kalland, David used the word translated "words" "for the revelation of God (Ps. 19)."[13] David asserted that the revelation of knowledge concerning God that comes through the heavens is worldwide in scope; it comes to every geographical area. As a result, no matter where people live on earth, they are exposed to this revelation. In line with this fact, Ralph H. Alexander wrote, "Creation itself gives a 'worldwide' witness to God's glory (Ps. 19:4) which should result in Yahweh's praise (Ps. 98:2)."[14]

The expression *their line is gone out through all the earth* contains an additional implication. In the Old Testament, the word translated "line" frequently referred to a measuring line, a standard by which other objects were measured (Isa. 34:17; 44:13; Jer. 31:39). Concerning this word, John E. Hartley stated, "A line is basically a measuring line. It stands parallel to plummet (Isa. 28:17)."[15]

In light of this concept, the additional implication of Psalm 19:4 is that the knowledge concerning God revealed worldwide through the heavens is the foundation for a world-life view. This foundation (the existence, wisdom, and power of one infinite, eternal God who created the universe) is the measuring line or standard by which the foundations of all other world-life views should be measured or evaluated. Any foundations that do not agree with this standard are contrary to reality, as are the views based on them.

In verses 4c and 5, David applied a twofold simile to the sun to illustrate the role it plays in the revelation of God through the heavens. First, the sun "is like a bridegroom coming out of his chamber." Here David borrowed from one aspect of Jewish marriage customs in Bible times. After the bride and bridegroom arrived at the house of the bridegroom's father on their wedding night, members of their wedding party escorted them to the bridal chamber *(huppah)*. While the groomsmen and bridesmaids waited outside, the bride and bridegroom entered the bridal chamber alone. There they consummated their marriage through physical union.[16]

After the marriage was consummated, the bridegroom came out of hiding in the bridal chamber to announce the consummation to the members of the wedding party waiting outside (Jn. 3:29).[17] Similarly, the sun, after hiding from view during the hours of darkness, comes out of hiding each morning as it appears over the eastern horizon to deliver an announcement. As it moves across the heavens from east to west, it announces the existence of the infinite, eternal God who had the power and wisdom to create it and place it in the heavens. The sun faithfully gives this witness to the entire world every day.

In the second simile, David declared that the sun "rejoiceth like a strong man to run a race." Runners, whose bodies have been trained to the peak of endurance, rejoice as they approach a starting line because they have the strength necessary to run a race. So the sun rejoices as it approaches the eastern horizon because it has the power necessary to race across the sky every day, giving its witness concerning God. The sun has such great power that "each day the earth receives in the form of solar energy about 200,000 times the total world electrical-generating capacity."[18] "The Sun converts five million tons of matter into energy every second."[19] In spite of this enormous conversion, it has the capacity "to shine for . . . 100 billion years at the present rate."[20]

Even a blind person who has never seen the sun is exposed to its witness concerning God. David said, "There is nothing hidden from the heat thereof" (v. 6). Thus there is no escaping the sun's witness in one way or another, be it through sight, heat, or its effects on all it touches.

David's statements in Psalm 19:1–6 indicate that there are no time, language, or geographical limits on this revelation of knowledge concerning God through the heavens. Regardless of historic time of life, language, or geographical location, every human being has been exposed to it. In addition, any world-life view that is not based on this revealed knowledge is contrary to ultimate reality.

Acts 14:15–17

As a result of the miraculous healing of a lame man through Paul's ministry, the pagan people of the city of Lystra concluded that Paul and Barnabas were gods and prepared to worship them (Acts 14:8–13). Horrified by what was about to happen, Paul and Barnabas prevented this worship by rushing in among the people, asserting that they themselves were only human. They exhorted the people to reject their idolatry, which was contrary to reality, and to turn to the God who exists, the God who created the universe and everything in it (vv. 14–15).

Paul and Barnabas told these people that in time past the true God did not force the Gentiles to walk in His ways. In other words, He did not put them under the restraint of the Mosaic Law, as He did the nation of Israel (Dt. 4:6–8; Rom. 2:14). Instead, He allowed them to conduct themselves according to their own ways (v. 16).

In verse 17, Paul and Barnabas hastened to add that although God dealt with the Gentiles in that manner in the past, He did not leave them without a witness concerning Himself. God gave evidence of His benevolent existence by doing good things for all humans, including pagan Gentiles, through nature—such things as giving them rain for their crops, fruitful seasons, fullness of food, and gladness. The word translated "gladness" sometimes referred to "the joy of the festive meal" and "can also be gratefully understood as the gift of God by which even the heathen may discern His providential rule."[21]

Romans 1:18–20

In this passage concerning God's revelation of knowledge about Himself through nature, Paul declared that God's wrath is being "revealed from heaven against all ungodliness and unrighteousness of men" (v. 18). The word translated "ungodliness" refers to the religious condition of those involved in false worship.[22] Paul equated this ungodliness with the "despising of God" that prompted ancient Greeks, Romans, and Egyptians to develop idolatrous religions (vv. 21–23, 25).[23] The word translated "unrighteousness" was equated with the "sexual and social perversion" or "unlawful conduct towards" other humans described in verses 24 and 26–32.[24]

The apostle indicated that the underlying cause of this false worship and perverted conduct was bias against the true God. People guilty of these actions possessed knowledge concerning God, but "they did not like to retain God in their knowledge" (v. 28); and they did not glorify Him as God or have an attitude of gratitude toward Him for His blessings (v. 21). The verb translated "did like" (v. 28) means "approve" and is equal to "intend, wish."[25] Thus Paul said these people did not approve of having God in their knowledge; therefore, they willfully intended to exclude His existence from their perception of reality.

That these people possessed knowledge concerning God but willfully intended to exclude His existence from their perception of reality indicates that they had a problem with their will, not their intellect. In other words, they did so not because intellectually they *could not* believe in the existence of God but because volitionally they did not *want* to believe in His existence. In spite of this fact, they tried to make it appear that they *had* to reject God's existence for intellectual reasons. They did so by asserting that they were wise to follow this action (v. 22) and thereby used the issue of intellect as a smoke screen to hide the real cause of their action.

Their willful rejection of God's existence prompted them to "hold the truth in unrighteousness" (v. 18). The word translated "hold" means "suppress"[26]

28

or "holding in prison."[27] In this passage, the word *truth* refers to "the 'revealed reality' of God."[28] Thus they were suppressing or holding in prison the reality of God that was revealed to them. A criminal is put in prison, away from society, so he cannot affect society and society does not have to be concerned about him. Likewise, these people imprisoned the revealed reality of God away from their perception of reality, so they could not be affected by it and would not have to be concerned about it.

The word translated "in" in the expression *in unrighteousness* means "with, by means of."[29] These people used unrighteousness as their means to imprison the revealed reality of God. This action indicates that the basis of their bias against God was their unrighteous philosophy of life, values, and lifestyle. They willfully rejected the reality of God's existence because His existence had serious implications concerning those areas of their lives, and they did not want to change them. Thus it was because of their morality and ethics, not intellect, that they rejected God's existence.

The word translated "because" at the beginning of verse 19 has strong "causal force."[30] Paul used it to introduce the major reason for God's wrath being revealed against the ungodliness and unrighteousness of the rejecters of His existence. They had no legitimate excuse for rejecting and ignoring His existence because He had clearly revealed it to them.

The word translated "known" in the phrase *that which may be known of God* refers to what is "capable of being known, intelligible"[31] or "recognizable."[32] It is singular in number and therefore refers to a body of knowledge concerning God that is intelligible to humans and capable of being known or recognized by them.

Paul declared that this body of knowledge "is manifest in them." The word translated "manifest" means "visible, clear, plainly to be seen, open, plain, evident, known."[33] It refers to "what can be perceived by the senses but in such a way that the perception involves understanding."[34] This body of knowledge was evident to its rejecters. It could be plainly seen or perceived by their senses to the extent that they could understand it and its implications for their lives.

They could plainly see this body of knowledge because "God hath shown it unto them." The verb translated "hath shown" has "causative significance" and means "to make visible what is invisible."[35] God took the initiative. He is invisible to mortal humans (Jn. 1:18; Col. 1:15; 1 Tim.

1:17), but He wanted His human creatures to know that He exists. As a result, He devised a visible way to reveal His existence to mortal man.

Paul explained how God revealed His existence to the rejecters: "For the invisible things of him from the creation of the world are clearly seen, being understood by the things that are made" (v. 20). God revealed knowledge concerning His invisible self through nature, the visible universe that He created.

The combination of the verb phrase *are clearly seen* with the expression *being understood* indicates that the seeing involved "an intellectual process."[36] Thus Paul was saying that God's "invisible nature is perceived with the eye of reason in the things that have been made."[37] In other words, as they observed nature, the rejecters intellectually perceived and understood the knowledge that God revealed about Himself through that means. Their problem was not an intellectual one.

Paul identified two invisible things concerning God that are revealed and clearly seen through nature: "his eternal power and Godhead." The word translated "Godhead" means "divinity, divine nature"[38] or "that which shows God to be God."[39] Thus, through nature, the existence of a being with a divine nature (God's existence) is revealed. God's eternal power is also revealed through nature. He had to have incredible power before the creation of the universe to bring it into existence.

Implications

Paul's language in Romans 1:18–20 implies several truths. First, the revelation concerning God through nature began at creation and continues throughout history to the present. Thus it has been intellectually perceptible to humans of all time periods, including the present.

Second, those who reject the existence of the eternally powerful God who created the universe do so because of a problem with their will, not their intellect. They do it, not because intellectually they *cannot* believe in God's existence but because volitionally they don't *want* to accept His existence because of the practical implications it will have for them. Thus they willfully suppress or imprison the knowledge of God that they perceive through nature, to keep it away from their view of reality. In actuality, then, their rejection of God is a moral or ethical, rather than an intellectual, issue.

Years ago an intelligent man told me he wanted to believe in Jesus Christ but couldn't for intellectual reasons. He had heard all the evidences and arguments in favor of belief but said that he would have to commit-intellectual suicide to believe the biblical claims concerning Christ.

On the basis of Romans 1:18–20, I told him, "Your problem is moral or ethical in nature, not intellectual. It is not that intellectually you *cannot* believe, but that volitionally you don't *want* to believe because of the implications it will have for you. You are using the intellectual as a smoke screen to cover up the real cause of your unbelief."

He got a smirk on his face and said, "You just put your finger on the nerve. I know that if I believe, I will have to change some practices in my vocation; and I'm not certain that I want to make those changes."

HISTORY

Events that will become historic, either in big or small ways, occur every day around all human beings everywhere on earth. Thus every person has been exposed to history, and God can use it to reveal truth about Himself to all mankind.

Biblical Examples

Several biblical passages indicate that God uses history to reveal knowledge about Himself.

First, in Exodus 7:4–5 God indicated that, through the judgments He would bring on Egypt in conjunction with Israel's exodus from that land, He would reveal truth about Himself to the Egyptians. The statements of Rahab, the Jericho harlot, in Joshua 2:9–11 demonstrate that God used His judgment of Egypt to uncover knowledge concerning Himself, even to the Canaanites.

Second, in Isaiah God called the nation Israel—"Israel, my glory" (46:13)—and stated that He created Israel for His glory (43:7) and "glorified Himself in Israel" (44:23). These statements indicate that through Israel, God manifests impressive truths about Himself to the rest of the world.

God reveals these truths through His historic dealings with Israel. In Deuteronomy 28 the Lord mapped out His future dealings with Israel from Moses' time to the Second Coming of the Messiah. In verses 1–14 God promised that, if Israel would heed His Word and obey Him, He would bless it more than any other nation. It would be the head nation above all others, not the tail nation.

By contrast, in verses 15–68 God warned that if the nation would reject His Word and disobey Him, it would be overtaken with many curses. He would bring oppressive enemies against the people and scatter them among all the nations. There they would have no permanent rest, would be gripped with fear and sorrow, and would have no assurance of life from day to day.

In verse 10 God stated the reason He would bless Israel above all nations if it would heed and obey His Word: "All people of the earth shall see that thou art called by the name of the LORD." In verse 37, He explained why Israel would experience many curses if it rejected and disobeyed His Word: "Thou shalt become an astonishment, a proverb, and a byword among all nations to which the LORD shall lead thee." These statements indicate that God uses His historic dealings with Israel as a means of impressing the world with two significant truths about Himself. First, He blesses those people who heed and obey His Word. Second, He curses those who reject and disobey His Word.

In light of this twofold revelational purpose of God's historic dealings with Israel and the intended worldwide audience of that revelation, it is no accident that God placed that nation in the most strategic geographical location on earth, both in ancient times and the 20th century. It is the crossroads of three of the world's great continents: Africa, Asia, and Europe. It also is no accident that, in the course of current events, the attention of the world is repeatedly drawn back to that nation.

Third, Daniel 4 records God's humiliation of Nebuchadnezzar, king of Babylon, the most powerful man of his day. Because of this ruler's arrogant pride, God inflicted him with mental illness that made him act like an animal. God's ultimate purpose for this historic happening was "to the intent that the living may know that the Most High ruleth in the kingdom of men, and giveth it to whomsoever he will, and setteth up over it the basest of men" (v. 17). In this instance God used history to reveal that He is the one who is in sovereign control of human affairs in this world.

Extrabiblical Examples

God has used historical happenings since Bible times to reveal to mankind His sovereign rule over human affairs. Two specific, extrabiblical examples illustrate this fact.

First, during the 16th century, the pope tried to force Protestant England back into the Roman Catholic Church through several means. He finally appealed to King Philip II of Spain to do the job for him by invading and conquering England. Spain was the greatest power in Europe and much of the world at that time.

Philip agreed to attack England. In the summer of 1588, the mighty Spanish Armada set sail from Spain with 131 ships and approximately 25,000 men. In several battles during one week, due to their expert seamanship and faster, more maneuverable ships, the English inflicted severe damage on the Spanish fleet but did not sink many of their ships. In a later battle they disabled or sank six Spanish ships and inflicted the loss of 4,000 men.[40]

The combination of fear and a strong wind drove the rest of the Armada north into the North Sea. The English fleet chased the Spanish until Queen Elizabeth ordered the navy home because of a storm.[41]

Because of the storm, the major part of the Armada escaped further damage by the English. "The storm, however, finished what the fleet had begun."[42] The Spaniards hoped to return home by rounding the north end of Scotland, but the storm shattered many of their ships on the rocky coasts of Scotland and Ireland. Thousands of men drowned. Many of those who reached shore were massacred. Less than half of the ships and about one-third of the men of the original Armada made it back to Spain.[43]

It was the storm, not the English, that inflicted the major damage to the Spanish naval power and thereby caused changes of major consequence. This was the beginning of the end for Roman Catholic Spain as a great world power. This event "established England as the champion of Protestantism in Europe and blasted the pope's last hope of regaining England for the Roman church."[44] It was a decisive blow to the militant thrusts of the Catholic Counter-Reformation against Protestantism and a tremendous boost to the Protestant cause in several European countries. It determined that Protestant England, not Roman Catholic Spain, would colonize most of North America and that colonial North America would be primarily Protestant rather than Catholic in faith.[45]

In light of these changes and the fact that God ultimately controls natural elements, I believe God's hand was moving through that storm to accomplish His purposes and thereby reveal to mankind His sovereignty over human affairs.

A second example of God's sovereign power was displayed when France fell to Hitler's forces in June 1940. Great Britain was "in a desperate situation. The internal defenses against a possible German invasion by sea were inadequate, there were not enough trained soldiers under arms and the supply of weapons was not sufficient."[46] It is estimated that, had Hitler given the command for his forces to invade England, that nation would have fallen in a week.[47] But "at the very moment when Hitler stood at the zenith of his military power, with most of the European Continent at his feet . . . he had no idea how to go on and bring the war to a victorious conclusion. . . . Hitler and his captains hesitated. They had not thought out the next step and how it was to be carried through. This fateful neglect would prove to be one of the great turning points of the war and indeed of the short life of the Third Reich and of the meteoric career of Adolf Hitler."[48] Hitler never commanded the invasion of England.

In May 1941, if he had followed the advice of several of his military leaders to take control of Egypt, the Suez, and the Middle East, "Hitler, with the use of only a fraction of his forces, could have dealt the British Empire a crushing blow, perhaps a fatal one."[49] But Hitler decided he had to destroy the Soviet Union first. William L. Shirer called this decision "a staggering blunder."[50]

In March 1941 Hitler made an emotional decision to postpone the Soviet invasion until after his forces had crushed Yugoslavia and Greece.[51] As a result, he did not launch the attack against the Soviets until five weeks after the original planned date.[52] This delay caused his forces to be devastated by the severe Russian winter. Shirer declared that this "was probably the most catastrophic single decision in Hitler's career."[53]

Who or what prompted Hitler to be indecisive and make disastrous decisions at critical times? I am convinced that God's hand was moving behind the scenes to destroy this tyrant and his evil system, thereby determining the outcome of World War II and revealing yet again His sovereign rule over mankind.

Limitations

God gives revelation through history, but people limit the effect of that revelation in at least two ways. First, many people, including Christians, do not like history; so they ignore it or try to change it. As a result, the lessons or truths God wants them to learn from history are lost to them. Second, the unsaved mind is so corrupted by sin that some people believe that other principles, such as fate, the survival of the fittest, or wealth, rather than God, are the ultimate determinants of historic events.

HUMAN CONSCIENCE

Paul referred to the human conscience in Romans 2:14–15. Every human is born with a conscience; therefore, God can use the conscience to reveal truths to all mankind. Through the conscience, God reveals that right and wrong actually exist and that humans are responsible for what they do and don't do. The conscience gives people a sense of guilt when they do something contrary to it and peace when they act in accord with it.

God's revelation through the conscience can be limited in two ways. First, by doing the same wrong repeatedly, people can sear their consciences (make them so insensitive to the wrong that it no longer bothers them, 1 Tim. 4:2). Second, human culture educates the conscience concerning the specifics of right and wrong. If culture has taught it concepts of right and wrong contrary to God's standards, then conscience will not be an accurate guide in every instance. In light of this fact, when people become saved, they may have to reeducate their consciences to bring specific concepts of right and wrong into conformity with God's standards (Rom. 12:1–2; Eph. 4:17—6:9).

CONCLUSION

Thus far in our study of divine revelation, we have seen that God uses three means of revealing knowledge to all mankind in general—nature, history, and the human conscience. Therefore, no one has a valid excuse for rejecting the reality of God's existence and other truths concerning Him.

SIGNIFICANCE OF GENERAL REVELATION

General revelation is God's uncovering of knowledge through means available to all mankind. He uses nature, history, and conscience as the major means of general revelation. This type of revelation has great significance for unsaved people, God, and Christians.

SIGNIFICANCE FOR THE UNSAVED

General revelation has a threefold significance for the unsaved.

Religious Nature of Man

General revelation explains the religious nature of most people in the world. Everywhere there are people who worship some being or thing. The Scriptures indicate that false religions are the result of unsaved reactions to, but perversion of, general revelation.

As noted in the previous chapter, in Romans 1 the apostle Paul discussed unsaved people who willfully reject the reality of God's existence, which is clearly revealed through general revelation to *all* mankind. They do not want to accept His existence because of the practical implications it will have on their unrighteous philosophy of life, values, and lifestyle. In other words, they reject God, not because intellectually they *cannot* believe in God's existence, but because volitionally they do not *want* to accept it (vv. 18–21). In spite of this fact, they try to make it appear that they *must* reject God's existence for intellectual reasons. Thus they assert they are wise to reject the reality that is clearly revealed through general revelation (v. 22).

But the rejection of reality is the pinnacle of stupidity, not wisdom; and it incites foolish actions (vv. 21–22). It prompts people to invent the lie that their existence and well-being depend on parts of creation rather than on the true Creator God. As a result, they mistakenly worship and serve different parts of creation instead of the God who created it (v. 25). In other words, they develop false religions.

Paul gave two examples of this foolishness—religions (such as those of ancient Greece and Rome) that worship images human in form and religions (such as those of ancient Egypt) that worship images of animals (v. 23). The current trends toward pantheism, nature worship, and the deification of man are other examples of false religions developing as the result of unsaved reactions to, but willful perversion of, the knowledge concerning God revealed through general revelation.

Knowledge to Seek God

General revelation gives unsaved people enough knowledge to prompt them to seek the true God but not enough to know Him personally or be saved. Paul indicated this fact in his address to the Athenian philosophers in Acts 17. After talking about the Creator God and significant things He has done for all mankind in general (vv. 24–26), Paul stated that God did these things so that "they should seek the Lord" (v. 27).

The fact that general revelation by itself does not give the unsaved enough knowledge to know God personally or be saved is evident from several biblical statements. Jesus declared, "I am the way, the truth, and the life; no man cometh unto the Father, but by me" (Jn. 14:6). Peter said concerning Jesus: "Neither is there salvation in any other; for there is no other name under heaven given among men, whereby we must be saved" (Acts 4:12). Paul clearly taught that, regardless of background, the only way a person can know the true God personally or be saved is through faith in Jesus Christ. In order to place his or her faith in Him, a person must hear the truth about Him (Rom. 10:9–15).

These statements strongly assert two truths. First, Jesus Christ is the *only* way to a personal, saving relationship with the only true God. He is not one of several ways. Second, unless people hear the truth about Jesus Christ and believe in Him, they cannot know the true God personally or be saved.

Although general revelation is given to all mankind, it does not contain or communicate the truth concerning Jesus Christ. Therefore, by itself it does not give enough knowledge for unsaved people to know God personally or be saved. The knowledge necessary for salvation is part of another kind of revelation—special revelation, which is God's revealing of knowledge through special means not always available to all mankind in general.

What can be said, then, about people who never hear about Christ? Are they really lost? Can God hold them responsible for their unbelief if they never receive the truth necessary for salvation?

It is my understanding that the answer to these questions is found in a principle derived from two incidents recorded in Acts. The first involved the Ethiopian eunuch (Acts 8). It is apparent that this man had been exposed to more than general revelation. The fact that he traveled from Africa to Jerusalem to worship indicates he had accepted Israel's God as the true God (v. 27). It also is apparent that he was responding properly to the revelation he had—he was seeking God even more by reading the Scriptures while returning home (v. 28). It should be noted, however, that this man had not heard the truth about Jesus Christ and, therefore, had not believed in Him for salvation (vv. 32–35).

Because he was responding properly to the revelation he had by genuinely seeking the true God, God responded by commanding Philip to travel to Gaza—a long distance from where he was conducting a success-ful evangelistic ministry in Samaria—to meet with this one man (vv. 26–29). Philip preached to him the truth concerning Jesus, and the man believed in Jesus and was baptized (vv. 35–38).

The second incident involved Cornelius, a Roman centurion who was stationed in Caesarea in Israel (Acts 10). It seems obvious that Cornelius had been exposed to some special revelation—no doubt through Jews in Israel—because, although he was an Italian Gentile, he had rejected the pagan worship of Rome and had become a devout worshiper of Israel's God as the true God (vv. 1–2). It also is obvious that he was responding properly to the revelation he had because he was seeking God by praying to Him "always" (v. 2). It should be noted, however, that Cornelius had not heard that the truth about Jesus Christ was for Gentiles; therefore, he had not believed in Him for salvation (11:13–14).

Because Cornelius was responding properly to the revelation he had by genuinely seeking God, God responded by sending an angel to instruct Cornelius to send for Peter, who would tell him how he could be saved (10:3–8; 11:13–14). Then God convinced Peter he should go to that Gentile's home (10:9–20). Peter began his message by declaring, "Of a truth I perceive that God is no respecter of persons," indicating that the truth about Christ was for Gentiles as well as Jews (vv. 34–35). Then he preached the truth about Christ, and Cornelius believed in Jesus for salvation, as evidenced by the fact that he received the Holy Spirit and was baptized (vv. 36–48).

It appears that a significant principle by which God operates can be perceived through these incidents. If people respond properly to the revelation they have received (whether general or special) by acknowledging the existence of the one true Creator God and seeking a personal relationship with Him, God will provide them with the additional special revelation (the truth about Jesus Christ) necessary for salvation, so they can believe and become saved. This principle is in line with Hebrews 11:6, which declares, "he that cometh to God must believe that he is, and that he is a rewarder of them that diligently seek him."

On the other hand, if people do not respond properly to the revelation they have received, God is not unjust or unfair if He does not provide them with the revelation necessary for salvation. Consequently, if people never hear the gospel of Jesus Christ, it is because they have not responded properly to the revelation they already have.

This perceived principle has a definite relationship to the third significance of general revelation for the unsaved.

No Excuse Before God

General revelation renders the unsaved without excuse before God. In Romans 1, after talking about the unsaved who willfully reject the reality of God's existence clearly revealed through general revelation to all mankind, the apostle Paul declared, "they are without excuse" (v. 20). Obviously this rejection by the unsaved is not a proper response to the revelation they have received; therefore, even if they never hear the truth about Jesus Christ, they have no valid excuse for their lack of salvation. Thus the unsaved who never hear the message of salvation are just as lost as those who do hear it but never believe.

Since all people everywhere throughout history have been exposed to general revelation, that revelation has the same threefold significance for every person who has ever lived.

SIGNIFICANCE FOR GOD

General revelation has a twofold significance for God.

Grace for All

First, general revelation gives God opportunity to bestow some aspects of His grace upon all mankind. Jesus declared that God "maketh his sun to rise on the evil and on the good, and sendeth rain on the just and on the unjust" (Mt. 5:45). In Acts 14:15–17 Paul and Barnabas stated that the true Creator God gives evidence of His benevolent existence by doing good things for all people, including unsaved Gentiles, through nature, such as giving them rain for their crops, fruitful seasons, abundant food, and gladness. (See also Acts 17:24–28.) Since these divine blessings through nature are common to all people, theologians have called these aspects of God's grace "common grace."

Justification for Judgment

Second, general revelation further justifies God's judgment of the unsaved who do not turn to Him. As noted earlier, the unsaved are without excuse if they do not respond properly to the general revelation given to them (Rom. 1:18–20).

SIGNIFICANCE FOR CHRISTIANS

General revelation has a twofold significance for Christians.

Common Ground With Unsaved

First, general revelation gives believers a point of contact or common ground with the unsaved when witnessing. Since all people have been exposed to general revelation, it is something Christians and unbelievers have in common from God. Therefore, it provides believers with a good starting point for witness, especially with unsaved people who have never been exposed to any kind of special revelation, such as the Scriptures. Paul used general revelation as the starting point of his witness to unsaved Gentiles in Lystra (Acts 14:15–17) and Athens (Acts 17:23–31) who did not have the Scriptures.

Confirmation of Faith

Second, general revelation confirms the faith of Christians. It reassures them that they have not placed their faith in cunningly devised fables. Their faith is based on reality and is, therefore, not in vain.

CONCLUSION

Because we are all exposed to general revelation, no one has an excuse not to seek the Creator. When we do seek Him, we will be provided with the revelation necessary for salvation through Jesus Christ.

CHAPTER FOUR

SPECIAL
REVELATION

Scripture indicates that God has used two major kinds of divine revelation to uncover truth to mankind: general and special. In earlier chapters we examined general revelation, which is God's uncovering of knowledge through means available to all mankind in general. This chapter addresses special revelation, which is God's uncovering of knowledge through special means not always available to all mankind.

General revelation can give limited knowledge of God. It does not, however, give more specialized knowledge, including the knowledge necessary for salvation. If people are to be saved, they must receive more knowledge about God than general revelation can offer. Therefore, special revelation is needed to provide the additional specialized knowledge.

MEANS OF SPECIAL REVELATION

God has used several special means to reveal knowledge to individuals or groups, some at certain times in history but not at other times.

Miracles

The Scriptures record many miracles that God performed Himself or enabled people to perform. For example, He parted the waters of the Red

Sea to enable the people of Israel to pass safely from Egypt to the Sinai Peninsula (Ex. 14). The walls of Jericho fell without the use of siege equipment (Josh. 6). Jesus healed many diseases (Mt. 9:35), and Paul healed a lame man (Acts 14:8–10).

Miracles reveal knowledge about God to people who witness them and those who hear or read about them. This means of special revelation has some limitations, however. Many people never witness a miracle. Oral and written accounts of miracles, unless divinely inspired, may be inaccurate. For example, the ancient Babylonian flood story appears to be an inaccurate account of the Noahic flood.

Dreams and Visions

In Bible times, God occasionally used dreams and visions to uncover knowledge. For example, through a dream given to Nebuchadnezzar, God revealed the course of Gentile world dominion from the time of ancient Babylon to the Second Coming of the Messiah and the future Kingdom of God (Dan. 2). By means of visions given to Cornelius the centurion and Peter, God clearly made it known that the gospel was to be taken to the Gentiles (Acts 10).

These means of revelation uncovered knowledge to the receivers of the dreams and visions and to those who heard or read about them, but they also had some limitations. God did not give everyone in Bible times a dream or vision. Dreams or visions could be misinterpreted; and oral and written accounts of them, like the miracles, could be unreliable if not divinely inspired.

Direct Speech

At times God imparted knowledge to people by speaking audibly to them. For instance, through direct speech God revealed specific knowledge to Noah concerning the flood and ark (Gen. 6:13—7:4) and clearly identified Jesus of Nazareth as the Son of God (Mt. 3:17; 17:5).

This means of revelation gave knowledge to the immediate hearers of the speech and those who were given oral or written accounts of the speech; but again, it had some limitations. God did not speak audibly to all people, and oral and written accounts of His speech could be inaccurate if not divinely inspired.

Angels

The Bible records several incidents of God sending angels to deliver specific revelations to people. For example, He sent the angel Gabriel to reveal to Daniel His long-range program for Israel and Jerusalem and the specific time when the Messiah would be in the world officially presenting Himself to Israel as its Prince (Dan. 9:20–27). God sent Gabriel to inform the virgin Mary that she was the woman whom He had chosen to give birth to the promised Messiah (Lk. 1:26–38). Plus an angel revealed to shepherds the birth and location of the Messiah (Lk. 2:8–12).

Revelation through angels revealed knowledge to the people to whom angels appeared and those who received oral and written accounts of the angelic messages. But this means of revelation has limitations too. Angels did not appear to everyone, and oral and written accounts of angelic messages could contain falsehood if not divinely inspired.

The Holy Spirit

God has delivered significant revelation through the Holy Spirit. For instance, through the Spirit He revealed to the apostles and New Testament prophets a body of knowledge that Paul called "the mystery," which was hidden from mankind prior to apostolic times (1 Cor. 2:6–10; cf. Eph. 3:3–9). Jesus declared that the Comforter—the Holy Spirit—would make the unsaved world aware of its sin, need for righteousness, and future judgment (Jn. 16:7–11). Jesus also indicated that during the corporate lifetime of His apostles who were with Him in the upper room, the Holy Spirit would uncover to them "all truth"—all the teaching that the Lord wanted the church to have (Jn. 14:26; 16:12–15). The Holy Spirit leads believers and gives internal witness that they are God's children and heirs (Rom. 8:14–17). The Spirit also testifies that eternal life is available through one source, Jesus Christ (1 Jn. 5:6–13).

Revelation through the Holy Spirit has come in varying degrees to believers and unbelievers. This means of uncovering knowledge also has some limitations, however. Left to himself, "natural man" (a person who is unsaved) does not accept the truth revealed through the Holy Spirit. That truth seems foolish to him. In addition, unsaved people are incapable of understanding that truth because, by themselves, they do not have the spiritual equipment necessary to understand it (1 Cor. 2:14). Believers also can resist the internal witness or prompting by the Holy Spirit (Eph. 4:30; 1 Th. 5:19), and it is possible to mistakenly interpret a purely emotional response as the prompting of the Spirit.

Prophecy

In Bible times, God uncovered knowledge through prophecies. Through the prophet Moses, for example, God revealed how He would deal with the nation of Israel throughout its history (Dt. 28—30). When the people of Israel cried out to God because of severe oppression by the Midianites, God sent them a prophet to reveal the reason for their suffering (Jud. 6:7–10). Through the prophet Agabus, God foretold the coming of a great famine in New Testament times (Acts 11:27–28).

Through prophecies, knowledge was uncovered to prophets and prophetesses, those who heard them prophesy, and those who were given oral or written accounts of the prophecies. This means of revelation also had some limitations. Not everyone in Bible times had access to a prophet or prophetess, and there were many false prophets and prophetesses who misled people (Jer. 14:13–15). If not divinely inspired, oral or written accounts of prophecies could be inaccurate.

Scriptures

The Scriptures are an extensive means of revelation of God's truth to mankind. They present all that people need to know about God to be saved, live godly lives, and minister effectively (2 Tim. 3:15–17). It is significant that the longest chapter in the Bible (Ps. 119) is devoted to the importance of the Scriptures. God required Israel's leaders to read and meditate on the Scriptures daily (Dt. 17:18–20; Josh. 1:8).

The Scriptures present a storehouse of knowledge to all people who hear or read them, but even this great means of divine revelation has limitations. Multitudes of people have never been exposed to any part of the Bible, and people who are illiterate cannot read the Bible. The work of translating, printing, and distributing Scripture is long, laborious, and costly; plus there are still many languages and dialects without any portion of it available. Even people who have access to the Bible in their language often ignore or misinterpret it.

Historical Life of Christ

The historical life of Jesus Christ on earth was an incredible revelation of God to mankind. John indicated this truth when he called Christ "the Word" (Jn. 1:1, 14). John's point was that Jesus Christ had the same function as words. Just as words are the outward expression of invisible thoughts, so Jesus Christ, through His life on earth, was the outward expression of invisible God the Father to mankind (Jn. 1:18; 1 Tim. 1:17).

Jesus indicated the same thing when He said, "He that hath seen me hath seen the Father" (Jn. 14:9). Paul taught that Jesus "is the image of the invisible God" (Col. 1:15); and the writer of Hebrews declared that Jesus, as God's Son, was "the brightness of his glory, and the express image of his person" (Heb. 1:3).

The historical life of Christ revealed great truths concerning God to the people who were eyewitnesses of Christ and those who have received oral or written accounts of His life. In spite of the greatness of this means of revelation, it, too, has some limitations. Multitudes of people have never heard or read about Jesus. Oral and written accounts of His life, unless divinely inspired, are unreliable. Many people misinterpret the person and work of Christ; and it is difficult for finite, mortal people to understand this unique God-Man.

Christian's Life

Since Christians, as God's spiritual children, have been made partakers of God's holy nature (2 Pet. 1:4), they are to reveal that nature to the world through their philosophy of life, values, and lifestyle (1 Pet. 1:14–16; 2:9–12). For this reason, Jesus said concerning believers, "Ye are the light of the world. . . . Let your light so shine before men, that they may see your good works, and glorify your Father, who is in heaven" (Mt. 5:14, 16). Paul told church saints that they are Christ's letter to the world, "known and read of all men" (2 Cor. 3:2–3). Someone has said that the only Bible some unbelievers will ever read is the life of a Christian. Another person has expressed it eloquently in a simple verse:

> You are writing a gospel, a chapter each day,
> In deeds that you do and words that you say.
> Men read what you write, whether false or true.
> Say, what is the gospel according to you?
>
> —Author unknown

47

The Christian's life can display truth concerning God to all believers and unbelievers who come in contact with or hear or read about a believer, but this means of revelation also has some limitations. In some parts of the world, people never meet a Christian. A Christian's improper conduct gives a perverted view of God to the world, and sometimes people misinterpret a believer's life. Oral and written accounts of a Christian's life can be inaccurate.

CONCLUSION

Through a variety of means—miracles, dreams and visions, direct speech, angels, the Holy Spirit, prophecy, Scriptures, the historical life of Jesus, and believers' lives—God has given us specialized revelation, including the knowledge we need to be saved.

Our lives can be powerful witnesses to God's salvation. What is yours telling the world about God?

CHAPTER FIVE

BIBLICAL VIEW
OF INSPIRATION

Thus far in our study of bibliology (the doctrine of the Bible), we have examined divine revelation, which involves God's uncovering of knowledge to mankind.

The next area of bibliology we will examine is divine inspiration, which involves the accurate presentation or recording of knowledge.

When God revealed knowledge to prophets and apostles in Bible times, it was their responsibility to present that knowledge to other people. Sometimes they did so through oral speech; at other times they presented it in written form. On still other occasions they did it both orally and in written form.

God was concerned that prophets and apostles present His revealed knowledge accurately since knowledge that is presented inaccurately is not the same knowledge. An inaccurate presentation of God's revealed knowledge would defeat the whole purpose of God's revealing it.

There was a problem, however. Left to themselves, prophets and apostles, like all other human beings, were fallible. If all they had to work with when it came time for them to present God's revealed knowledge to other people were their natural abilities, then they were bound to be inaccurate in their presentations on occasion.

How could God prevent the prophets and apostles from inaccurately presenting the knowledge He revealed to them? He did it by the Holy Spirit working with them, giving them supernatural enablement when it was time for them to make their presentations. This guaranteed that what they spoke and wrote was accurate, or inspired.

The Bible claims to be divinely inspired—the accurate, written record of knowledge God wanted mankind to have. In making this claim, Scripture presents seven principles that together constitute the biblical view of what is involved in inspiration. All seven of these principles are vitally important. Any view that does not include all of them is a misrepresentation and perversion of the biblical view.

This chapter states and explains the seven principles. Later chapters will present biblical evidences for them.

SEVEN PRINCIPLES OF INSPIRATION

Divine Authorship

Inspiration involves divine authorship of the Scriptures. The Bible is the result of divine activity. God, not mankind, is its ultimate source; therefore, the Bible is God's Word to mankind. Apart from God the Scriptures would have been far different from what they are.

The key term for this first principle is *divine authorship*.

Divine Authority

Inspiration guarantees the divine authority of the Scriptures. Because the Bible is God's Word to mankind, it is the declaration of the will and purpose of the Creator, sovereign Lord, and Judge of the whole universe for mankind. Thus the Bible is fully and divinely authoritative over all mankind believes and does. Consequently, every human being should pay careful attention to the content of the Bible and bring his or her philosophy of life, value system, and conduct into conformity with its teaching. Those who do not do so will suffer serious consequences.

The key term for this second principle is *divine authority*, which some theologians call *infallibility*.

Verbal Inspiration

Inspiration resides in what was written, even in the very words written. God inspired every word of the original Scriptures.

Inspiration must go further than the mental or written thoughts of the human writer. The fact that a person has an accurate thought in mind does not guarantee he or she will present that thought accurately to other people. People who have done public speaking or writing know there are times when they do not say or record what they intended to speak or write. In spite of the fact that they had in mind the exact words they wanted to use to express their thoughts, for some unexplainable reason they left out some of those words or used words they never intended. There is many a slip between the mind and the mouth or pen.

Accurate thoughts require accurate words for accurate expression. For Scripture to be an accurate record of accurate thoughts, every written word had to be inspired by God.

The key term for this third principle, the concept that every word of the Bible was inspired, is *verbal inspiration*.

Plenary Inspiration

Inspiration affects all of the Scriptures. Every part of the Bible is inspired, and every part is inspired equally.

This principle rules out false views that state that only those parts of the Bible that deal with matters of faith and practice were inspired and therefore are free from error, that those parts of the Bible related to historical events and scientific matters were not inspired and therefore are subject to error, and that there are different degrees of biblical inspiration with some parts being more inspired than others. Therefore, freedom from error depends on the degree of inspiration. Those parts that are more inspired are less susceptible to error, and those parts that are less inspired are more susceptible to error. All three of these views violate the biblical view of inspiration.

Because this fourth principle emphasizes the fact that the whole Bible is inspired and inspired equally and because the word *plenary* means *entire* or *complete*, the key term for the fourth principle is *plenary inspiration*.

Inerrancy

Inspiration guarantees the inerrancy of the Scriptures, meaning the Bible was written without any error. Everything in it was recorded accurately.

The key term for this fifth principle is *inerrancy*.

Human Factors

Inspiration involved the use of human factors in the writing of the Bible. Each human writer employed human activity and used such things as his own personality, intellect, training, abilities, personal interests, literary style, and cultural background. For example, Isaiah, who was highly educated, used the fullest and richest Hebrew vocabulary of any of the Old Testament writers. In addition, books of the Bible exhibit various literary styles.

Combining this principle with the earlier ones prompts the conclusion that both human and divine factors were involved in writing the inspired Scriptures. The Bible is the result of divine revelation and enablement working together with the human factors noted above. Some theologians have called this combined activity *concursive operation*. As a result of this operation, the Scriptures ended up being God's Word in human language that human beings could understand.

A few, small portions of the Bible were produced by human writers recording what God dictated to them. The fact, however, that the human factors noted above were involved in writing the Bible indicates that the overwhelming majority of the Scriptures was not the result of divine dictation to the human writers. Only God, with His infinite intelligence and wisdom, could work with human writers in such a way that, while using their own human factors, they would write exactly what He wanted written, apart from dictation.

The key term for this sixth principle is *human factors*.

Original Autographs

God inspired the original autographs of the Scriptures. It was absolutely crucial that the original Scriptures be divinely inspired. Just as streams of water cannot be pure if their original source is impure, so copies and translations of the Scriptures cannot have God's full, divine authority if their original autographs were not divinely inspired.

None of the original autographs of the Bible is available today, however. This fact troubles some people. Because God is sovereign over what happens in the world, they reason, He could have prevented the original autographs from disappearing. The fact that He didn't indicates He had a purpose for permitting them to disappear. Perhaps He did so to prevent us from regarding the original autographs as sacred relics to be worshiped. Such worship would be idolatrous since only deity is to be worshiped.

People should not be troubled because none of the original autographs is available today. Over the centuries the Scriptures have been carefully copied and translated into many different languages. The history of this meticulous preservation of the content of the original Bible is fascinating. As a result of this careful work, the Scriptures that are available today are still the authoritative Word of God to mankind.

It should be noted that the original autographs of the Old Testament were not available in the first century A.D. In spite of this fact, Jesus Christ, the apostles, and the New Testament regarded the Old Testament Scriptures that were available at that time as the authoritative Word of God. Therefore, it is not necessary to have the original autographs available in order to have the authoritative Word of God.

The key term for the seventh principle is *original autographs*.

DEFINITION OF DIVINE INSPIRATION

Several scholars have developed definitions of divine inspiration as it relates to the Bible. One of the best I have seen was devised by Dr. Kenneth Kantzer (presented in his course on revelation and inspiration at Wheaton Graduate School during the school year of 1958–59). The strong feature of this definition is that it incorporates all seven principles that together constitute the biblical view of what is involved in inspiration. Here is his definition:

Inspiration is the work of the Holy Spirit by which, through the instrumentality of the whole personality and literary talents of its human authors, He constitutes the words of the Bible in its entirety as His written word to men, and therefore of divine authority and without error in the original manuscripts.

CHAPTER SIX

SCRIPTURE'S WITNESS CONCERNING ITS INSPIRATION: ITS HUMAN NATURE

Both human and divine factors were involved in the writing of the inspired Scriptures. This fact means that the Bible, as the written Word of God, has both a divine and human nature, just as Jesus Christ, as the living Word of God in the world, had both a divine and human nature.

This chapter presents the Bible's witness concerning some aspects of its human nature.

HUMAN PURPOSES AND METHODOLOGY

According to the Scriptures, some writers employed human purposes and methodology in the production of their biblical writings. We shall examine two examples.

Luke 1:1–4

After referring to other prepared accounts of the earthly life and ministry of Jesus Christ (vv. 1–2), Luke stated:

It seemed good to me also, having had perfect understanding of all things from the very first, to write unto thee in order, most excellent Theophilus, That thou mightest know the certainty of those things, wherein thou hast been instructed (vv. 3–4).

The words translated "it seemed good to me also" convey the meaning "I decided."[1] The language indicates that Luke purposed on his own to write his Gospel.

Luke's goal was to write his account "in correct chronological order,"[2] so his reader, Theophilus, would know the certainty of the things he had been taught about Christ.

In order to accomplish this goal, Luke carefully investigated everything related to Christ's life and ministry before he began to write his Gospel. From the beginning of his investigative activity, he was careful to be accurate (the word translated "understanding" means to "investigate a thing,"[3] and the word translated "perfect" means "accurately, carefully"[4]).

It is interesting to note that Luke is the only Gospel writer who recorded the circumstances related to John the Baptist's birth, angel Gabriel's visit to Mary, Mary's innermost feelings in response to that visit, Mary's visit to Elisabeth, and the angelic announcement of Christ's birth to the shepherds. How did Luke obtain his information concerning these events and the responses of the people involved in them? He must have personally interviewed Mary, Elisabeth, and perhaps some of the shepherds as part of his investigative activity.

These details indicate that Luke obtained the information he recorded in his Gospel through hard research and study. It did not come to him through divine revelation. In other words, he employed human methodology, using his human abilities.

Although Luke had his own purpose for writing his Gospel and employed human methodology in gathering his materials, the Bible's witness concerning its divine nature prompts two conclusions. First, as Luke sorted through his gathered information, the Holy Spirit guided him in his choices of what to record and what to leave out. Second, during the writing process the Spirit worked with him in such a way that he recorded everything accurately.

John 20:30–31

Toward the end of his Gospel, the apostle John wrote, "And many other signs truly did Jesus in the presence of his disciples, which are not written in this book; But these are written, that ye might believe that Jesus is the Christ, the Son of God; and that believing ye might have life through his name."

John thereby indicated he had his own purpose for writing his Gospel—bringing his readers to eternal life by convincing them to believe the truth that Jesus of Nazareth is the true Messiah and the Son of God. In order to accomplish his purpose, out of an abundance of material available to him (see 21:25), he carefully selected only those items that would suit his purpose, implying human methodology.

Concerning John's statements in these verses, Leon Morris wrote,

In this statement of intention John first makes it clear that in his Gospel he has made a selection. He has not by any means written all that he knows about Jesus. . . . He has written what served his purpose and has omitted much. . . . Now John gives us the purpose of his book, that purpose which he has had steadily in mind from the beginning. . . . He tells us that the purpose of his writing is that men may believe. . . . He has not tried to write an impartial history. He is avowedly out to secure converts.[5]

USE OF UNINSPIRED SOURCES

Several writers of biblical books recorded information derived from pieces of literature that were not divinely inspired. The fact that they did so indicates they obtained these materials through personal research, rather than by divine revelation. The following examples demonstrate the use of such uninspired sources.

1 and 2 Chronicles

The writer of 1 Chronicles declared,

Now the acts of David, the king, first and last, behold, they are written in the book of Samuel, the seer, and in the book of Nathan, the prophet, and in the book of Gad, the seer, With all his reign and his might, and the times that went over him, and over Israel, and over all the kingdoms of the countries (29:29–30).

The books of Samuel, the seer; Nathan, the prophet; and Gad, the seer, apparently were historical records of King David's deeds written by these three prophets, who had close associations with him. The Israelites never recognized their books as divinely inspired and, therefore, did not include them in the canon of the Scriptures. The fact that the writer of 1 Chronicles referred to those books at the end of his own book implies that he used them as sources of information for what he wrote.

The writer of 1 Chronicles also referred to genealogical records of the tribes of Israel that provided him with information (4:33; 5:17; 7:9, 40; 9:22). Concerning these sources, C. F. Keil wrote,

These genealogical lists were most probably in the possession of the heads of the tribes and families and households, from whom the author of the Chronicle would appear to have collected all he could find, and preserved them from destruction by incorporating them in his work.[6]

The same writer quoted directly from royal letters of King Sennacherib of Assyria (2 Chr. 32:17) and a written royal proclamation of King Cyrus of Persia (36:22–23). He also derived much of his information concerning various kings of Judah from "the book of the kings of Israel and Judah" (2 Chr. 27:7; 35:27; 36:8), the official court records of the reigns of Judah's kings.[7]

Concerning the use of these and other uninspired sources by the writer of 1 and 2 Chronicles, J. Barton Payne made the following significant comments:

That the Chronicler used many sources does not mean that these were "lost biblical books" but merely indicates the honest research he conducted in writing his inspired account. Nothing in the Chronicler's remarks need be construed as suggesting that the canon is incomplete or that the entirety of the sources named here was inspired.[8]

1 and 2 Kings

It appears that the writer of 1 and 2 Kings used at least three uninspired royal annals or records as sources of information for his inspired books: "the book of the acts of Solomon" (1 Ki. 11:41), "the book of the chronicles of the kings of Judah" (1 Ki. 14:29; mentioned 15 times in 1 and 2 Kings), and "the book of the chronicles of the kings of Israel" (1 Ki. 15:31; mentioned 17 times in 1 and 2 Kings).[9]

2 Samuel

The writer of 2 Samuel quoted a strongly emotional poem that David wrote as a lament over the deaths of King Saul and Jonathan (1:17). The content of the poem is presented in its entirety in verses 19–27. The writer indicated that he derived this poem from "the book of Jasher" (v. 18). Also mentioned in Joshua 10:13, the book of Jasher "is thought to have been a collection of poetry, probably odes and psalms in praise of

Israel's heroes and exploits."[10] Some scholars believe it was lost during the Babylonian Captivity.[11]

Numbers

In Numbers 21:14–15 Moses quoted a portion from "the book of the wars of the Lord." Jewish scholars believe this ancient book "contained songs celebrating the victories of the Israelites led by YHWH."[12] For example, the portion that Moses quoted refers to the victory God gave the Israelites over Egypt at the Red Sea.

Jude

In verses 14–15 Jude recorded a statement either from the book of Enoch or the oral tradition of Enoch's declarations.[13] The original Hebrew text of the book of Enoch "was written by the Chasidim or by the Pharisees between 163–63 B.C." and was "a collection of apocalyptic literature written by various authors and circulated under the name of Enoch."[14] Although the Jewish people highly regarded it, they never recognized it as divinely inspired and, therefore, never included it in the canon of Scripture.

The fact that several writers of biblical books recorded information derived from uninspired sources prompts a question. In the previous chapter we examined seven principles that constitute the biblical view of inspiration. One of those principles was the following: Inspiration guarantees the inerrancy of the Scriptures, meaning the Bible was written without any error. By contrast, uninspired literature can contain error. In light of this contrast, does the biblical writers' use of uninspired sources jeopardize the inerrancy and, therefore, the inspiration of Scripture?

The answer to this question is that the use of uninspired sources does not jeopardize the inerrancy and inspiration of the Scriptures if the writers used parts of those sources that were not erroneous. It is essential to note that although uninspired writings can contain error, not everything in that kind of literature is erroneous. It is my conviction that the Holy Spirit guided the writers of Scripture to use only those parts of uninspired sources that were free from error.

Edward C. Pentecost gave a specific example of this answer. He indicated that Jude's use of an uninspired source does not affect "the doctrine of inspiration adversely. If Jude quoted the apocryphal book, he was affirming only the truth of that prophecy and not endorsing the book in its entirety."[15]

INDIVIDUAL LITERARY STYLE AND VOCABULARY

Each writer of the Scriptures employed his own literary style and vocabulary, which were distinct from those of the other writers. A prime example was the prophet Isaiah, as noted by Israel W. Slotki's comments:

Scholars pay wholehearted tribute to Isaiah's brilliance of imagination and his picturesque and graphic descriptions, his command of powerful metaphor, alliteration, assonance, and the fine balance of rhythmic flow of his sentences. His poetical diction is superb, and every word of his kindles, stirs and strikes its mark. His thought constantly and spontaneously blossoms into imagery, and the images are no mere rhetorical embellishments but are always impressive in themselves and always appropriate and natural expressions of his ideas.[16]

Victor Buksbazen stated,

Isaiah was endowed with a superb mastery of language, which was concise, colorful, harmonious and effective. . . . With the talent of a great master, he always manages to make his visions or thoughts come to life with vivid and bold strokes. No other prophet was able to conjure up before the eyes and ears of his listeners such a vivid sense of the awesome majesty of God's presence as did Isaiah. . . . Isaiah is justly considered the greatest of all the writing prophets.[17]

CONCLUSION

Although the Bible is divinely inspired, God used human beings to write it. Therefore, it reflects a variety of human purposes, methodologies, literary styles, and vocabularies.

CHAPTER SEVEN

SCRIPTURE'S WITNESS CONCERNING ITS INSPIRATION: ITS DIVINE NATURE

Both human and divine factors were involved in the writing of the inspired Scriptures. The previous chapter presented the Bible's witness concerning some aspects of its human nature; this one will present the Bible's own witness concerning its divine nature.

APOSTLES' WITNESS CONCERNING THE DIVINE NATURE OF THE OLD TESTAMENT

Apostle Paul's Witness

In 2 Timothy 3:16 Paul wrote, "All scripture is given by inspiration of God." This statement is certainly true of the Old and New Testaments, but in this context Paul applied it primarily to the Old Testament. We know this fact from his comment to Timothy in the preceding verse: "And that from a child thou hast known the holy scriptures, which are able to make thee wise unto salvation through faith which is in Christ Jesus" (v. 15). Gottlob Schrenk wrote that in this passage the expression *the holy Scriptures* "refers to the OT as a whole."[1] Very little, if any, of the New Testament had been written and distributed when Timothy was a child.

Several significant facts should be noted concerning Paul's statements. First, He ascribed divine inspiration to "all" of the Old Testament. He hereby asserted that the entire Old Testament in all its parts was inspired by God. Schrenk declared that Paul's expression *all scripture* "obviously means every passage of Scripture."[2]

Earlier in this study I noted that one of the seven principles that together constitute the biblical view of inspiration is plenary inspiration. The word *plenary* means "entire or complete." Thus plenary inspiration means that every part of the Bible is inspired and is inspired equally. Paul's statement in 2 Timothy 3:16 is one of several from which the concept of plenary inspiration is derived.

Second, the word translated "given by inspiration of God" is comprised of two parts. The first part, *theo*, comes from the Greek word for God. The second part, *pneustos*, comes from the Greek word for breath, wind, or spirit. Thus, the entire word means "God-breathed." Paul said that the entire Old Testament in all of its parts was God-breathed.

When Paul declared that all of the Old Testament was God-breathed, he did *not* mean that God breathed something supernatural into it *after* it had been written by its human writers. For example, after Moses had finished writing Deuteronomy, it did not become divinely inspired as the result of God's reading it and becoming so impressed that He decided to breathe a supernatural quality into it.

Paul did mean that God was breathing out the Scriptures while the human writers were writing them. In other words, God, not the human writers, was the ultimate source or author of the Old Testament Scriptures. He was the primary person responsible for bringing the Scriptures into existence.

One of the seven principles of biblical inspiration presented earlier stated that inspiration involves divine authorship of the Scriptures. The Bible is the result of divine activity. God, not mankind, is its ultimate source; therefore, the Bible is God's Word to mankind. Second Timothy 3:16 is a significant source of this principle of divine authorship.

Third, according to Paul it was the Scriptures, not human writers, that were inspired by God. In other words, through inspiration it was the written Scriptures, not the human writers, that God was breathing out or bringing into existence. For example, God was not breathing out Moses or bringing him into existence when Moses was writing Deuteronomy.

Moses had already been in existence for many years before he wrote that book. The Holy Spirit worked supernaturally with human writers while they were writing the Scriptures; but, in light of Paul's statement, it is not accurate to say the writers were inspired while writing. Later we shall see that the Bible uses a different term for the supernatural working of the Spirit with the human writers.

Fourth, the fact that the second part of the word translated "given by inspiration of God" comes from the Greek word for breath, wind, or spirit indicates that the Holy Spirit was the divine agent involved in the inspiration of the Old Testament Scriptures.

Fifth, in his 2 Timothy 3:15 statement to Timothy, Paul called the Old Testament Scriptures "holy." In the Bible the word *holy* is applied to items that, because of their relationship with God, are different, distinct, or unique in contrast with common, ordinary things. Paul said that the Old Testament Scriptures are different, distinct, or unique in contrast with all nonscriptural writings. They are so because they were inspired (breathed out) by God.

By contrast, all nonscriptural writings are common or ordinary because they were not inspired by God. Human writers were their only source. Concerning Paul's application of the term *holy* to the Old Testament Scriptures, Eduard Schweizer wrote, "It is thus evident that the author is differentiating the writings ordained by God's authority from other, secular works."[3]

On the basis of these five observations, we conclude that in 2 Timothy 3:15–16 Paul gave significant apostolic witness concerning the divine nature of the Old Testament. Indeed, as Gottlob Schrenk wrote, "The true doctrinal formulation of inspiration is most comprehensively given in 2 Tim. 3:16."[4]

Apostle Peter's Witness

After referring to the subject of salvation in the preceding verse, Peter wrote the following:

> *Of which salvation the prophets have inquired and searched diligently, who prophesied of the grace that should come unto you, Searching what, or what manner of time the Spirit of Christ who was in them did signify, when he testified beforehand the sufferings of Christ, and the glory that should follow* (1 Pet. 1:10–11).

Peter's statement concerns future prophecies that the Old Testament prophets wrote about the Messiah. In spite of the fact that they wrote those prophecies, they did not understand them. This lack of understanding indicates the prophets were not the ultimate source of what they wrote. Peter asserted that the Holy Spirit was the ultimate source, working supernaturally in the writers to produce those prophecies. Peter thereby gave apostolic witness concerning the divine nature of Old Testament Scriptures.

In another passage, 2 Peter 1:20–21, after telling his readers that they had better pay attention to the Scriptures written by Old Testament prophets (v. 19), Peter wrote, "Knowing this first, that no prophecy of the scripture is of any private interpretation. For the prophecy came not at any time by the will of man, but holy men of God spoke as they were moved by the Holy Spirit."

Through these statements, Peter told his readers they had better pay attention to the Scriptures that the Old Testament prophets wrote because the *ultimate source* of those Scriptures was God, not the human prophets who wrote them. Peter asserted that the foremost truth to know about those Scriptures was their source.

When the apostle stated that "no prophecy of the scripture is of any private interpretation," he was not talking about the explanation or understanding of Scripture. Instead, he was referring to the ultimate source of the Scriptures written by the Old Testament prophets. Two things tell us this.

First, the root of the word translated "interpretation" means "set free, release."[5] A more literal translation of Peter's statement is, "Every prophecy of scripture became [came into being] not of one's own releasing." Peter was indicating that the Old Testament prophets were not the ultimate ones releasing or bringing into existence the Scriptures they wrote.

Second, Peter began his next statement (v. 21) with the word *for*. It indicates that verse 21 explains what he meant by the statement translated "no prophecy of the scripture is of any private interpretation." A more literal translation of verse 21 is, "For no prophecy was ever made by will of man, but men spoke from God while being moved by the Holy Spirit."

This explanation clearly indicates that Peter emphasized the ultimate source of the Scriptures written by Old Testament prophets. God, not the prophets, was that source. The prophets were the vehicles through whom God produced the Old Testament Scriptures by means of the Holy Spirit working supernaturally with the prophets while they wrote.

Instead of saying the prophets were inspired, Peter declared that they were "moved" by the Holy Spirit while they wrote. The word Peter used meant "be moved, be driven."[6] In light of this fact, Konrad Weiss wrote that the prophets "spoke as they were 'impelled' by the Holy Ghost."[7]

The word translated "moved" was used in biblical times for the activity of the wind moving or driving a sailing ship through the water (Acts 27:15, 17).[8] This choice is interesting in light of two facts: the Greek word for the Spirit also means "wind," and Jesus used the activity of the wind as a simile for the activity of the Spirit when He talked with Nicodemus (Jn. 3:8).

A comparison of the activity of the wind moving a ship through the water with the activity of the Holy Spirit moving the Old Testament prophets to write divinely inspired Scripture prompts an interesting analogy. Just as a sailing ship had its own man-made equipment, such as a hull, masts, crossbars, rigging, and sails, so the prophets had their own human factors, such as personality, intellect, vocabulary, training, abilities, personal interests, literary style, and cultural background.

In the same manner that a sailing ship—in spite of all its man-made equipment—could never move itself through the water, so the prophets—in spite of all their own human factors—could never produce divinely inspired Scripture by themselves.

Just as a sailing ship was totally dependent on the wind to provide the power to move it through the water, so the prophets were totally dependent on the Holy Spirit to provide the supernatural influence needed to write the divinely inspired Scripture. This indicates that deity was the ultimate source of the Scriptures that Old Testament prophets wrote.

In the same manner as the wind blew into the ship's sails and thereby made use of its man-made equipment to move it through the water, so the Holy Spirit made use of the prophets' human factors to produce divinely inspired Scripture in human language that human beings could understand. Thus both divine and human factors were involved in the writing of inspired Scripture. The Bible is the result of divine revelation and enablement working together with human factors.

Peter's explanation in 2 Peter 1:21 is the closest the Bible comes to describing the means or how of the inspiration of Scripture.

THE OLD TESTAMENT'S WITNESS CONCERNING ITS DIVINE NATURE

More than two thousand times, the Old Testament claims to be the record of what God has said to mankind. We will take a few examples of this witness from the three major divisions of the Hebrew Old Testament: The Law (Torah)—Genesis, Exodus, Leviticus, Numbers, Deuteronomy; The Prophets (Nebhiim)—Joshua, Judges, Samuel, Kings, Isaiah, Jeremiah, Ezekiel, The Twelve; and The Writings (Kethubhim)—Psalms, Proverbs, Job, Song of Songs, Ruth, Lamentations, Esther, Ecclesiastes, Daniel, Ezra, Nehemiah, and Chronicles.

The Law

Exodus 24:4 states, "And Moses wrote all the words of the LORD." Fifty-four times the book of Numbers declares it is the record of what God said to Moses.

The Prophets

Twenty times the book of Isaiah claims it presents God's Word (e.g., Isa. 1:2, 10).

The book of Jeremiah makes the same claim about 100 times. For example, Jeremiah wrote, "Then the word of the LORD came unto me" (1:4); and he declared, "Then the LORD put forth his hand, and touched my mouth. And the LORD said unto me, Behold, I have put my words in thy mouth" (1:9).

The book of Ezekiel asserts, "The word of the LORD came expressly unto Ezekiel, the priest, the son of Buzi, in the land of the Chaldeans by the river, Chebar; and the hand of the LORD was there upon him" (1:3). At least 44 times Ezekiel declared that the Word of the Lord came to him.

Nearly all of the minor prophets claimed they were presenting God's Word. In fact, in their opening verses, Hosea, Joel, Micah, Zephaniah, Haggai, Zechariah, and Malachi all indicated they were communicating "the word of the Lord" that came to them.

The writer of 1 Kings testified concerning the divine nature of the book of Joshua. He recorded the fulfillment of a warning that was "according to the word of the LORD, which he spoke by Joshua, the son of Nun" (1 Ki. 16:34).

The prophet Daniel gave witness regarding the divine nature of the book of Jeremiah. He wrote, "I, Daniel, understood by books the number of the years, concerning which the word of the LORD came to Jeremiah, the prophet, that he would accomplish seventy years in the desolations of Jerusalem" (Dan. 9:2).

The prophet Zechariah testified concerning the divine nature of the writings of the prophets who ministered before the Babylonian Captivity of the Jewish people. Referring to the rebellious attitude of precaptivity Jews, he declared,

Yea, they made their hearts as an adamant stone, lest they should hear the law, and the words which the LORD of hosts hath sent in his Spirit by the former prophets; therefore came a great wrath from the LORD of hosts (Zech. 7:12).

The Writings

King David, "the sweet psalmist of Israel, said, The Spirit of the LORD spoke by me, and his word was in my tongue" (2 Sam. 23:1–2). David thereby claimed divine inspiration for his psalms.

CHRIST'S WITNESS CONCERNING THE DIVINE NATURE OF THE OLD TESTAMENT

Jesus Christ gave many lines of witness concerning the divine nature of the Old Testament.

Indestructibility of the Law

First, in Matthew 5:18 He said, "For verily I say unto you, Till heaven and earth pass, one jot or one tittle shall in no way pass from the law, till all be fulfilled." The "jot" is the *yod*, the smallest letter in the Hebrew alphabet. It is similar in size and shape to our apostrophe. The "tittle" is only a very small part of a Hebrew letter. Through these terms, Jesus emphasized the most minute parts of the Law division of the Hebrew Old Testament.

Kenneth L. Barker, explaining the significance of Christ's statement, asserted,

[The Lord] set forth the indestructibility of the law in its smallest details. The inviolability of all of God's revelation in the Scriptures is, by implication, likewise upheld. The importance of such a minute detail as a yod can be accounted for only by recognizing that Christ regarded the individual words of Scripture as inspired and authoritative, for the change of a letter might well change the whole word and its meaning.[9]

Through His statement Jesus indicated that divine inspiration of the Law division of the Old Testament went even deeper than individual words. It extended to the smallest letters and parts of letters within words. Christ believed in even more than verbal inspiration for the Old Testament.

He began His statement with the expression, *For verily I say unto you.* It was used in ancient times to call attention to a solemn statement that is "reliable and true."[10] Jesus thereby emphasized the reliability and truthfulness of His statement concerning the Law division of the Old Testament.

Submission to the Old Testament

Second, when Satan tempted Jesus, the Lord did not use His miraculous powers as His weapon against the Devil and his temptations. Instead, He used the Scriptures like a sword. He reached into the Old Testament, took the passage that fit the nature of each temptation, and thrust it at the Devil by speaking it to him (Mt. 4:4, 7, 10).

Christ's action on that occasion was most significant. Even though He was the Son of God—absolute deity incarnated in human flesh—He submitted Himself to the authority of the Old Testament, the only Scriptures written at that time. He would not violate those Scriptures, thereby bearing witness to the absolute divine authority of the Old Testament.

Authority of the Law

Third, in Mark 7:6–13 Christ rebuked the Pharisees and scribes for laying aside what Moses wrote—the Law division of the Old Testament—in order to keep man-made traditions.

Two things should be noted concerning this rebuke. First, Jesus equated what Moses wrote in the Law with "the commandment of God"

(vv. 8–9) and "the word of God" (v. 13). He thereby testified concerning the divine inspiration of the Law division of the Old Testament.

Furthermore, through this rebuke Christ indicated that the Scriptures have authority over man-made tradition. He did not say that all man-made tradition is wrong. He did, however, make it clear that any tradition that is contrary to the Scriptures must be rejected. He thereby gave witness to the divine authority of the Law division of the Old Testament.

Divinely Inspired

Fourth, Christ declared that David wrote Psalm 110:1 by the Holy Spirit (Mk. 12:36). He thereby claimed divine inspiration for that Old Testament passage.

Fulfillment of Prophecies

Fifth, referring to a statement in Isaiah 53:12, Jesus said, "This that is written must yet be accomplished in me" (Lk. 22:37). He thereby indicated that the event foretold in this Old Testament passage *had* to be fulfilled. The only possible reason for this necessity of fulfillment would be divine revelation and inspiration of that passage. Writings totally human in origin do not have to be fulfilled. Thus, Jesus' statement implied the divine nature of that Old Testament passage.

Plenary Inspiration

Sixth, in Luke 24:25 Jesus declared, "O foolish ones, and slow of heart to believe all that the prophets have spoken!" Jesus quickly followed up this statement with the following action: "Beginning at Moses and all the prophets, he expounded unto them, in all the scriptures, the things concerning himself" (v. 27). This action indicates that He was equating the entire Old Testament with "all that the prophets have spoken."

Several things should be noted regarding Christ's statement and action. The expression *foolish ones, and slow of heart* refers to people "lacking understanding or judgment."[11] Thus Christ said that when people do not believe the entire Old Testament, it is because they lack understanding or judgment. Also, Christ began His statement with the emotional interjection "O," indicating that He is disturbed when people do not believe all of the Old Testament.

The Lord's statement indicates that people should believe not just some but "all" of the Old Testament. There can be only one legitimate reason for such all-inclusive belief: the divine inspiration of the entire Old Testament. Thus Christ's statement revealed His belief in the plenary inspiration of the Old Testament.

Divine Revelation

Seventh, in Luke 24:44 Jesus said, "All things must be fulfilled, which were written in the law of Moses, and in the prophets, and in the psalms, concerning me." He thereby claimed that everything written about Him in all three divisions of the Hebrew Old Testament *had* to be fulfilled. The only possible reason for this necessity of fulfillment would be divine revelation and inspiration of the content of these divisions. Thus Christ's statement implied the divine nature of all the Messianic passages throughout the entire Old Testament.

No Error

Eighth, after quoting an Old Testament statement, Jesus declared, "The scripture cannot be broken" (Jn. 10:35). The word translated "broken" means "repeal, annul, or abolish."[12] Leon Morris indicated that Jesus' statement "means that Scripture cannot be emptied of its force by being shown to be erroneous."[13] Thus Jesus insisted that it is impossible for people to free themselves of personal responsibility to the teaching of Scripture by asserting that it is in error. Scripture has serious implications for all human beings, implications they cannot abolish.

The only way Christ's declaration could be true is if the ultimate source of Scripture is God. Because Jesus said this in conjunction with an Old Testament passage, He thereby affirmed the divine authority and truthfulness of the Old Testament.

God's True Word

Ninth, Jesus said to God, "Thy word is truth" (Jn. 17:17). Jesus used the term *word* to refer to God's revelation given to mankind.[14] This revelation would include, but not be limited to, the Old Testament. Indeed, in Mark 7:6–13 Jesus equated Old Testament Scripture with "the word of God."

70

According to Merrill C. Tenney, the unusual construction of the expression translated "thy word" "implies that the 'word' is peculiarly God's; it originates from him and is qualified by his personality."[15] Because the term *word* referred to revelation that included the Old Testament, Jesus thereby indicated the divine source of the Old Testament.

Jesus equated God's Word with "truth." Leon Morris indicated that He thereby was saying the following: "Divine revelation is eminently trustworthy. . . . The Father's Word, all that He has revealed, is of the same kind. It is truth and may therefore be unhesitatingly accepted and acted upon."[16] Jesus asserted the complete trustworthiness of all divine revelation, including the Old Testament.

CHRIST'S WITNESS CONCERNING THE DIVINE NATURE OF THE NEW TESTAMENT

Jesus' Promise of the Spirit

The night before He was crucified, Jesus informed His apostles of something that disturbed them greatly. In a little while He would leave them to return to His Father's house in heaven (Jn. 13:33—14:2).

Jesus relieved the apostles' fears by promising that they would not be abandoned like orphans during His absence. God the Father would give them another Comforter, the Holy Spirit, to replace Jesus' presence with them (Jn. 14:16–17).

Christ's comments indicated that, after His return to the Father in heaven, the Holy Spirit would be related to the apostles in a way in which He had not been related to them before (Jn. 14:17). On the day of His ascension, Jesus told the apostles that this new relationship with the Holy Spirit would begin in Jerusalem "not many days from now" (Acts 1:5). It began 10 days later on the Day of Pentecost (Acts 2:1–4).

Activities of the Spirit

John 14:26. On the night before His crucifixion, Jesus foretold various ways in which the Holy Spirit would be involved with the apostles. Among those ways was the following: "But the Comforter, who is the Holy Spirit, whom the Father will send in my name, he shall teach you all things, and bring all things to your remembrance, whatever I have said unto you" (Jn. 14:26). This statement is extremely significant because it has two implications concerning the divine nature of the New Testament.

First, Jesus indicated that everything He had taught the apostles before His ascension would be brought to their remembrance by the Holy Spirit after His ascension. This activity of the Holy Spirit has a tremendous implication concerning the divine nature of the New Testament. The Gospels profess to be the record of Jesus' teaching that He gave during His years of ministry with the apostles. Two of the Gospels, Matthew and John, were written by two of Jesus' apostles. Neither of these Gospels was written until several decades after Jesus' ascension. Thus they profess to record teaching given by Jesus many years earlier. Because human beings quickly forget and often have faulty memories of things they have been taught, on what basis can we trust the accuracy and reliability of these Gospel accounts of Jesus' teaching?

Jesus Himself revealed the basis of that truth. He indicated that after His ascension, the Holy Spirit would bring to the apostles' remembrance "all things" that He had taught them during His years of ministry with them. He was telling them that the Holy Spirit would play a significant role in the apostles' oral and written accounts of Jesus' teaching, working supernaturally with those men to produce accurate, reliable documents. Thus before any of the New Testament was written, Jesus bore witness in advance to the divine nature of the Gospels of Matthew and John.

The second implication is contained in the Lord's declaration that the Holy Spirit "shall teach you all things." This statement indicated that the teaching He had already given the apostles before His ascension was not complete. Much more truth was to be taught to the apostles for the benefit of the church, but the Holy Spirit would communicate it to them after Christ's ascension.

Christ stated that the Holy Spirit would teach those men "all things," not just some things. Because Jesus declared this to the apostles who had been with Him during His years of earthly ministry and because they were His apostles to the church (1 Cor. 12:28; Eph. 4:11–12), He thereby indicated that all the teaching He wanted the church to have would come during the corporate lifetime of those men.

This fact does not mean they were the only ones to whom the Spirit would communicate additional teaching for the benefit of the church. Paul was neither saved nor an apostle when Jesus said this. Once Paul became an apostle, he received teaching through the Spirit, as did New Testament prophets (1 Cor. 2:6–13; Eph. 3:2–5). But it does mean that before the last of them would die, the corporate body of apostles who had been with Christ before His ascension would receive all of the teaching He wanted the church to have. It is no accident, then, that John, the last of the apostles to die, wrote the last book of the New Testament only a few years before his death. Revelation is the capstone of all the teaching Christ had for the church.

This activity of the Holy Spirit—teaching "all things" to the apostles— has an important implication concerning the divine nature of the New Testament. The apostles and New Testament prophets recorded that additional teaching in the Epistles and Revelation. Thus when Jesus declared this future activity of the Holy Spirit, He indicated that the Spirit would be the ultimate source or author of those books of the New Testament. Before any of the New Testament was written, Jesus thereby witnessed concerning the divine nature of the Epistles and Revelation.

John 16:13. On the night before His crucifixion, Jesus once again foretold ways in which the Holy Spirit would be involved with the apostles after His ascension. He told them, "I have yet many things to say unto you, but ye cannot bear them now" (Jn. 16:12). Apparently the teaching He had already given them had brought them to the saturation point. This condition posed a problem. Because He had told them that He would be leaving them shortly, how would they obtain the additional knowledge He wanted them to have?

Jesus presented the solution to this problem when He declared, "Nevertheless, when he, the Spirit of truth, is come, he will guide you into all truth; for he shall not speak of himself, but whatever he shall hear, that shall he speak; and he will show you things to come" (Jn. 16:13).

In the first part of this declaration, Jesus asserted that the Holy Spirit would guide His apostles into "all the truth" (literal translation), not just some of it. Thus, once again the Lord indicated that during the corporate lifetime of the apostles who had been with Him during His earthly ministry, all of the additional truth He wanted the church to have would be delivered to them by the Spirit.

Jesus also stated that the Holy Spirit would show the apostles "things to come" (future events). Prophecies concerning the future were recorded in some of the Epistles and most of Revelation.

Through both parts of this declaration, Christ once again witnessed ahead of time concerning the divine nature of the Epistles and Revelation. The Holy Spirit would be their ultimate source.

THE APOSTLES' WITNESS CONCERNING THE DIVINE NATURE OF THE NEW TESTAMENT

Apostle Paul's Witness

Paul witnessed concerning the divine nature of the New Testament in 1 Corinthians 2:13. In verse 10 he referred to things God had revealed to the apostles and New Testament prophets by the Holy Spirit (cf. Eph. 3:5, where Paul talked about knowledge "which in other ages was not made known unto the sons of men, as it is now revealed unto his holy apostles and prophets by the Spirit").

In verse 13 Paul explained what happened when the apostles and New Testament prophets communicated this Spirit-revealed knowledge: "Which things also we speak, not in the words which man's wisdom teacheth, but which the Holy Spirit teacheth, comparing spiritual things with spiritual." The word translated "comparing" also means "combine."[17] The first word translated "spiritual" "can denote the content of the knowledge given by God's Spirit."[18]

Paul said that when the apostles and New Testament prophets communicated the knowledge revealed to them by the Holy Spirit, the Spirit worked with them supernaturally, enabling them to combine Spirit-revealed thoughts with Spirit-prompted words. In other words, their verbal communication of God's revelation was divinely inspired; the Spirit even inspired the words. This action was necessary if their communication was to be accurate. Accurate thoughts require accurate words for accurate communication.

Because the apostles and New Testament prophets communicated God's revelation—not only orally but sometimes in written form—this activity of the Spirit took place when they wrote the books of the New Testament. Thus in his 1 Corinthians 2:13 statement, Paul claimed divine inspiration for the words of those books and thereby witnessed concerning the divine nature of the New Testament. This passage is a significant basis for the concept of verbal inspiration.

74

In 1 Corinthians 14:37 Paul asserted, "The things that I write unto you are the commandments of the Lord," thereby indicating that God was the ultimate source or author of what he wrote in 1 Corinthians. This statement was his witness for the divine nature of that book.

Apostle Peter's Witness

Peter claimed that when Paul wrote his epistles, he recorded "the wisdom given unto him" (2 Pet. 3:15). He thereby indicated that Paul was not the ultimate source or author of his epistles.

Peter referred to certain people who abused Paul's epistles, "as they do also the other scriptures, unto their own destruction" (2 Pet. 3:16). Through this statement, Peter put Paul's epistles in the category of Scripture.

Because the apostles applied the term *Scriptures* exclusively to divinely inspired writings (2 Tim. 3:16), Peter thereby claimed divine inspiration for Paul's epistles. His assertion that abuse of Paul's epistles would bring destruction indicated that those New Testament books were not just human writings.

CONCLUSION

Why is belief in the divine inspiration of the Bible important? One critical reason is, as noted, that Jesus Christ believed and taught the divine inspiration of the Old and New Testaments. In light of this fact, denying the divine inspiration of the Bible is defaming the character and truthfulness of Jesus Christ. If He knowingly taught error on this subject, then He lied and thereby flawed His character. If He taught error because of personal ignorance, how can we be certain He didn't do the same thing on other subjects? Denial of the divine inspiration of the Bible prompts conclusions and questions such as these and thereby undermines the person and work of Jesus Christ.

THE
PERSONAL WORD
OF GOD

CHAPTER EIGHT

JESUS CHRIST'S NAMES AND TITLES

In the first section of this book, we examined the first major area of doctrine—Bibliology, the study of the Bible. This chapter begins an examination of another significant area—Christology, the study of Christ.

A consideration of some of Jesus Christ's names and titles is a good place to begin the study of Christology. In biblical times names and titles had great significance. They were designed to reveal such aspects as a person's nature, character, position, and accomplishments. Thus a study of Christ's names and titles reveals significant information concerning Him.

Lord

Lord was used to signify two characteristics of Christ. The Greek word for lord *(kurios)* means "master or sovereign." Thus sometimes it was used as a title to reveal that Christ is the Master or Sovereign Lord over all of creation. Peter seemed to have this meaning in mind when he asserted that Jesus Christ "is Lord of all" (Acts 10:36).

In addition, this term was used to reveal Christ's deity. During the course of Old Testament times, Jews came to regard God's personal name *Yahweh* (written JHVH) as too sacred to pronounce because it signified His absolute deity. Abraham Cohen explained it this way:

To the Oriental, a name is not merely a label as with us. It was thought of as indicating the nature of a person or object by whom it was borne. For that reason special reverence attached to "the distinctive Name" of the Deity which He had revealed to the people of Israel, viz. the tetragrammaton, JHVH.[1]

Thus whenever Jews came to that name in their Hebrew Scriptures, they pronounced a substitute title. "Instead of JHVH the Name was pronounced *Adonai.*"[2] *Adonai* means "lord, master, or sovereign."

Consequently, when Jewish scholars produced the Septuagint (the Greek-language version of the Hebrew Old Testament) during the 200s and 100s B.C., they used *kurios* (lord), the Greek counterpart of the Hebrew title *adonai*, as the substitute for Yahweh.[3] By New Testament times the title *kurios* (lord) was commonly used as a substitute for God's personal name *Yahweh* and, when so used, was intended to communicate the idea of absolute deity. Thus, on many occasions, the early church used the title *Lord* (*kurios*) to signify the absolute deity of Jesus Christ. The fact that the blind man whom Christ healed worshiped Him when he called Him "Lord" (Jn. 9:38) indicates he used that term to signify Christ's deity.

Jesus

Jesus is Christ's human and historical name. He did not have this name before He became a human being through His incarnation. The angel told Joseph, "Thou shalt call his name JESUS" (Mt. 1:21, future tense).

In addition to signifying Christ's humanity, this name identified a major aspect of His ministry. Jesus means "Yahweh saves"; thus this name revealed that Christ would do the work of salvation for mankind. The angel gave the reason for His human name: "for he shall save his people from their sins" (Mt. 1:21).

Christ

Christ is the Greek and New Testament counterpart of the Hebrew and Old Testament title *Messiah*. Concerning Andrew's statement, "We have found the Messiah," the New Testament asserts, "which is, being interpreted, the Christ" (Jn. 1:41). The terms *Christ* and *Messiah* mean "anointed one." Thus this title signifies that Jesus of Nazareth is the one God specially anointed to do His work, accomplish God's purpose for history, and fulfill the Old Testament Messianic prophecies.

Immanuel (Emmanuel)

This name emphasized the deity of Jesus Christ. It indicated that He was God dwelling in the midst of the people of Israel. The angel who spoke to Joseph concerning Jesus said, "They shall call his name Immanuel, which, being interpreted, is God with us" (Mt. 1:23). Jesus clearly demonstrated that He was "God with us" when He allowed the Shekinah glory to radiate through His human flesh at His transfiguration (Mt. 17:1–6). The Shekinah glory always signified the unique presence of deity.

The Son of God

John the Baptist gave the following witness concerning Jesus: "And I saw, and bore witness that this is the Son of God" (Jn. 1:34). The combination of the definite article *the* and the singular form of *Son* in this title is significant. It reveals that Christ is the Son of God in a unique sense.

The Old Testament calls angels "the sons of God" (Job 1:6) because He brought them into existence through creation, but Christ was not created. The New Testament calls believers "the sons of God" (Jn. 1:12–13, KJV) because they became His spiritual offspring through the new birth, but Christ did not need the new birth. Thus Christ is the Son of God in a unique sense that is not true of angels or human believers. This fact is emphasized even more by His enlarged designation "the only begotten Son of God" (Jn. 3:18).

The uniqueness of Christ's Sonship in relation to God the Father is revealed by the fact that in the Old Testament and writings of postbiblical Judaism, the Hebrew words for "son" were "often used to denote the relationship which determines the nature of a man."[4] Thus the title *the Son of God* signified that Christ had the same divine nature as God the Father. Because of this fact, the Jews recognized that, when Christ claimed to be the Son of God, He was ascribing absolute deity to Himself (Jn. 5:17–18; 10:33, 36).

The title *the Son of God* also indicated that Christ is a separate person from the Father (Mt. 3:16–17; Jn. 5:19–22) and is the heir, not the servant, of the Father (Mt. 21:33–39; Heb. 3:5–6).

The Son of Man

Son of Man emphasized Jesus Christ's humanity (Lk. 9:58). As a result of His incarnation, Christ became a human being with a complete human nature. The combination of the definite article *the* plus the singular form of "son" is significant. It reveals that Christ is the unique offspring of humanity. All other human offspring are sinful by nature, but Christ is sinless in His humanity (Jn. 8:46; Heb. 4:15). In addition, He is the only human being who can accomplish the victory of humanity over its enemies (Heb. 2:14–17).

As the Son of man, He died as our substitute and rose bodily from the dead to save sinful people (Lk. 9:22; 19:10). At His Second Coming He will return as the Son of man to rule the earth (Mt. 24:29–30; 25:31–34).

The Last Adam

Jesus Christ is "the last Adam," the counterpart of the first Adam (1 Cor. 15:45). Through his original rebellion against God, the first Adam caused the theocratic Kingdom of God to be lost from the earth, the world system to come under Satan's rule, and nature to be subjected to a curse (Lk. 4:5–6; Rom. 8:20–23). At His Second Coming Christ will return to the earth as "the last Adam" to end Satan's rule, restore God's theocratic Kingdom-rule to the earth, and remove the curse from nature (Rev. 19:11—20:6; Mt. 19:28).

The Word

The apostle John called Jesus Christ "the Word" (Jn. 1:1, 14). This title refers to an important function that Christ had in the world during His first advent. A person's thoughts are invisible to other people unless those thoughts are given outward expression. The instrument used for this expression is words, either in spoken or written form. Thus words are the outward expression of invisible thoughts to people.

By analogy, the Bible teaches that God the Father is invisible to mortal human beings (Jn. 1:18; 1 Tim. 1:17). It also indicates that, while Jesus Christ was on the earth, He was the outward expression of God to people (Jn. 1:18; Col. 1:15; Heb. 1:3). When Jesus was asked to show the Father to His disciples, He said, "He that hath seen me hath seen the Father" (Jn. 14:8–9). Just as words are the outward expression of invisible thoughts to people, so Jesus Christ was the outward expression of the invisible Father to them. He was the personal revealer of God to mankind.

Light of the World

Christ was called "the Light" (Jn. 1:7–9), and He called Himself "the light of the world" (Jn. 8:12). Light's function is to expose what is hidden; therefore, this title signified several characteristics of Christ. First, He was the revealer of God and His truth to mankind (Jn. 8:26). Second, He looks inside people to expose their innermost beings (Jn. 1:9). He did this to Nathanael (Jn. 1:47–48) and the scribes and Pharisees (Lk. 6:6–8). Third, He exposes the outward deeds of people (Jn. 3:19–21); He did this to the Samaritan woman at Jacob's well (Jn. 4:16–19).

Lamb of God

John the Baptist said of Jesus, "Behold the Lamb of God, who taketh away the sin of the world" (Jn. 1:29). The combination of the definite article *the* with the singular form of "Lamb" is significant. It implies that Christ was unique in His function as a sacrificial lamb in at least three ways. First, the Jews were required to provide their own lambs as sacrifices for their sins. By contrast, Christ was the Lamb that God, not human beings, provided.

Second, the Jews were required to offer many lambs as repeated sacrifices for their sins. God offered only one Lamb, His Son, as a onetime sacrifice for mankind's sin (Heb. 9:28; 10:11–12). Third, the many lambs the Jews offered could not take away sins (Heb. 10:11). The onetime sacrifice of Christ took away the sin of the world (Heb. 10:10).

King of Israel

Nathanael said to Jesus, "thou art the King of Israel" (Jn. 1:49). The Old Testament foretold that in the future the Messiah, a physical descendant of King David, would rule the nation of Israel as the heir of David's ruling authority (2 Sam. 7:16; Isa. 9:6–7; Jer. 23:5–6), as well the entire world (Zech. 14:9).

Centuries later the angel Gabriel told the virgin Mary this about Jesus, the unique Son to whom she would give birth: "The Lord God shall give unto him the throne of his father, David. And he shall reign over the house of Jacob forever; and of his kingdom there shall be no end" (Lk. 1:32–33).

Gabriel thereby revealed that Jesus Christ is that promised King of Israel, the Messiah, who will fulfill the Old Testament prophecies by ruling with His ancestor David's authority over the nation of Israel throughout the Millennium and eternity in the future.

King of Kings and Lord of Lords

Jesus Christ will have the title of King of kings and Lord of lords on His garment and thigh when He comes out of heaven in His Second Coming to end Satan's rule over the world system and restore God's theocratic Kingdom-rule on the earth (Rev. 19:16). During the future reign of Christ there will be distinct nations with individual kings and other ruling authorities. But Jesus Christ will be the ultimate King over all these other kings and the ultimate ruling authority over all other ruling authorities (Ps. 72:10–11, 17; Zech. 14:16–19).

CONCLUSION

This list of names and titles is not exhaustive. Other designations are given in the Bible; however, these give significant insight into the person and work of Jesus Christ. They indicate that He was and is a unique person who came in the past and will come again in the future to do a unique work.

CHAPTER NINE

JESUS CHRIST'S ETERNALITY AND PREEXISTENCE

Although Jesus Christ was born in a human body at a specific point in time, He existed before that event. In fact, He has always existed, having no beginning and no end. In other words, Christ is preexistent and eternal. In this chapter, we'll explore these two attributes.

ETERNALITY

Christ's eternality deals with the fact that He has always existed as a person from eternity past with no beginning and no end. The Scriptures give at least three lines of evidence for this fact: direct biblical statements, the deity of Christ, and His role in creation.

Direct Biblical Statements

Four biblical passages clearly ascribe eternality to Christ. The first, Micah 5:2, declares that Judah's future deliverer, who would rule in Israel on God's behalf, would be born in the small town of Bethlehem. Because humanity is born and deity is not, this part of the declaration revealed that the Messiah would be a human being.

The next part asserted that this same person's "goings forth have been from of old, from everlasting." Concerning this statement, D. K. Innes wrote, "These words are suited to convey both the ancient lineage of Christ as a descendant of the family of David and also His eternal pre-existence."[1] Because eternal existence is an attribute of deity, but not of humanity, this part of the declaration ascribed deity to the Messiah.

Thus Micah 5:2 indicates the Messiah would be a God-Man, a unique being with deity and humanity existing in the same person. His humanity would have a beginning through conception and birth; but as a divine person, He is eternal—without beginning.

Note two facts regarding this prophecy. First, in spite of the fact that Jesus Christ's mother and stepfather lived in the city of Nazareth (Lk. 1:26–33), He was born in Bethlehem (Lk. 2:1–7) in fulfillment of Micah 5:2, as the result of an imperial decree of Rome.

Second, the ancient Jews understood that Micah 5:2 referred to the Messiah. This is revealed by these events: Wise men from the east came to Jerusalem and asked King Herod, "Where is he that is born King of the Jews?" Herod asked the chief priests and scribes where the Messiah should be born. They answered, "In Bethlehem of Judea," and quoted Micah 5:2 as their proof (Mt. 2:1–6).

The second biblical passage that contains a direct statement about the eternality of Christ is Isaiah 9:6. In a context describing the future rule of the Messiah, this verse applies the name "the Everlasting Father" to Him. Franz Delitzsch stated that this name designated the Messiah "as the possessor of eternity" and as the one who would rule His people like a loving, faithful father.[2]

The third direct statement passage is John 1:1–3. Referring to Christ as "the Word," the apostle John stated, "In the beginning was the Word. . . . The same was in the beginning with God" (vv. 1–2). He thereby asserted that Christ already existed with God before everything that had a beginning first began. Christ existed in eternity past before any part of creation came into existence. Concerning John's statement, Leon Morris wrote, "The verb 'was' is most naturally understood of the eternal existence of the Word."[3]

The fourth biblical passage is Hebrews 7:3. The writer declared that Christ had "neither beginning of days nor end of life." Concerning this declaration, Leon Morris stated, "The writer is, of course, speaking of the Son's eternal nature, not of his appearance in the Incarnation."[4]

Deity of Christ

The deity of Christ is the second line of evidence for His eternality. Deity's nature is to be eternal. Thus the apostle Paul signified that eternality is one of God's attributes (1 Tim. 1:17). The Scriptures present the deity of Christ; therefore, He, too, must be eternal by nature. The biblical evidence for Christ's deity will be examined in a later chapter.

Christ's Role in Creation

The apostle John asserted the following truth concerning Christ: "All things were made by him; and without him was not anything made that was made" (Jn. 1:3). Christ played a significant role in the creation of everything that has ever been created. That work required His existence in eternity past before creation began. If Christ had not existed before the beginning of creation, He could not have been involved in the creation of everything that has ever been created.

The apostle Paul declared the same truth about Christ when he wrote, "For by him were all things created . . . all things were created by him, and for him; And he is before all things" (Col. 1:16–17).

Concerning John's and Paul's statements about Christ, Herbert M. Carson said, "Here it is the Son in His eternal being who is being described, rather than the Son as incarnate. In fact, there is a close parallel between this passage and John's teaching concerning the eternal Word or *Logos*. The only-begotten is also the agent of creation. . . . Far from being in any way a part of creation, the Son is *before all things*. . . . He is eternal, while creation is in time."[5]

Firstborn of All Creation

In Colossians 1:15 the apostle Paul referred to Christ as "the first-born of all creation." Some individuals and groups insist that this designation indicates Christ was the first part of creation that God brought into existence. They claim that Paul taught that Christ is a created being, that He had a beginning in time and therefore is not eternal.

Does the expression "the first-born of all creation" mean that Christ was the first thing created? No, it does not. Paul was *not* saying that Christ is a created being. Several facts prompt this conclusion.

First, Paul wrote Colossians to refute a heresy (Gnostic Judaism) that taught that Christ was part of creation.

Second, the idea that Christ was created is contrary to the context of Paul's reference to Christ as "the first-born of all creation." The context teaches that Christ created everything that has been created (vv. 16–17). Thus F. F. Bruce wrote, "The context makes it clear that this title is not given to Him as though He Himself were the first of all created beings; it is emphasized immediately that, far from being part of creation, He is the One by whom the whole creation came into being."[6]

Third, there was a Greek word (protoktistos) that meant "first-created." Paul did not use it here, and it is never used of Christ in the Bible.

Fourth, the word Paul did use (prototokos) had two connotations: priority and sovereignty. Priority had two possible subconnotations: the first part of something or existence before something. The context of the word determines which subconnotation is intended. The Colossians 1 context demands the subconnotation of existence before something else. Verses 16 and 17 clearly indicate that Christ existed "before all things" that were created. Thus, when Paul referred to Christ as "the first-born of all creation," he was teaching that Christ existed before and is sovereign over all of creation. F. F. Bruce stated, "What the title does mean is that Christ, existing as He did before all creation, exercises the privilege of primogeniture as Lord of all creation, the divinely appointed 'heir of all things' (Heb. 1:2). He was there when creation began, and it was for Him as well as through Him that the whole work was done."[7]

PREEXISTENCE

Preexistence and eternality are not necessarily the same. This is evident because a human being can exist before a certain event, but that does not mean he or she is eternal by nature. Thus when reference is made to the preexistence of Christ, the emphasis is not necessarily on His eternality. Instead, it is on the fact that He existed before His incarnation in human flesh. He existed before He was born of the virgin Mary.

There are several evidences for the preexistence of Christ.

Eternality of Christ

Several lines of evidence have been examined for the fact that Christ is an eternal being, without beginning or end. The fact that He is eternal by nature prompts the conclusion He existed before His incarnation.

Christ's Claim of Preexistence

On one occasion when Christ was confronted by enemies, He said, "Your father, Abraham, rejoiced to see my day; and he saw it, and was glad" (Jn. 8:56). His enemies challenged Him by saying, "Thou art not yet fifty years old, and hast thou seen Abraham?" (v. 57). Jesus responded with an astonishing claim: "Verily, verily, I say unto you, Before Abraham was, I am" (v. 58). The word translated "was" in this statement literally means "became or came to be" and refers to Abraham's birth.[8]

Thus, through that statement, Christ claimed He existed before Abraham was born. In light of that claim, the fact that Abraham lived approximately 2,000 years before Christ's incarnation forces the conclusion that Christ existed before His own human birth. The fact that Christ used the word *verily* twice at the beginning of His claim signifies He was emphasizing the reliability and truthfulness of His claim of preexistence.

Preincarnate Appearances of Christ

The Old Testament Scriptures refer to a being who, on several occasions, either appeared or spoke to human beings. Various titles were applied to this being, such as "the angel of the Lord," "the angel of God," and "the captain of the host of the Lord." The Old Testament references reveal that this being was divine, not an angel. The word translated "angel" in the Bible literally means "messenger" and sometimes refers to beings other than angels.

An example of an appearance by this being is recorded in Exodus 3—4. The person who appeared to Moses in the burning bush is called "the angel of the Lord" (3:2); however, He is identified as "the LORD" and "God" (3:4) and "I am" (3:14). He claimed to be "the God of Abraham, the God of Isaac, and the God of Jacob" (3:6). Moses hid his face from this being "for he was afraid to look upon God" (3:6).

These statements signify that a divine being appeared to Moses. Because the Scriptures clearly teach that no mortal human has ever seen God the Father (Jn. 1:18; 6:46), we must conclude that this divine being was not the Father. The Bible also indicates that Christ is the being who reveals God to the world (Jn. 1:18; 14:8–9; Col. 1:15; Heb. 1:3). It seems evident, then, that Christ was the being who made these appearances to

Moses and others in Old Testament times. These appearances testify to His preexistence before His incarnation in human flesh.

CONCLUSION

Christ's existence did not begin when He was conceived in Mary's womb and born into the world several months later. As an eternal, divine being, He had always existed without beginning and end throughout eternity past and Old Testament history. When, at a specific point in time, He was incarnated in human flesh, He added a complete human nature to His preexistent, eternal, divine nature. The Word, who existed with God the Father before the beginning of creation, became flesh and dwelt among people on the earth for more than 30 years (Jn. 1:1–3, 14).

CHAPTER TEN

JESUS CHRIST'S DEITY

Jesus of Nazareth was a divine being in human flesh. Although many people deny this fact, there is plenty of evidence for His deity. This chapter explores some of this evidence.

Old Testament

Two Old Testament passages that ascribed deity to the Messiah will be noted. Isaiah 9:6 assigned the names "The Mighty God, The Everlasting Father" to the Messiah. Ancient Judaism recognized that this verse referred to the Messiah. The Aramaic *Targum Jonathan* (first century B.C.) paraphrased part of Isaiah 9:6 as follows: "And there was called His name from of old, Wonderful, Counsellor, Mighty God, He who lives for ever, the Messiah in whose days peace shall increase."[1]

Both Isaiah and Jeremiah indicated that "mighty God" (*El Gibbor*) was a name of God (Isa. 10:21; Jer. 32:18). Thus Isaiah 9:6 ascribed deity to the Messiah when it said that this name of God would be His name.

Franz Delitzsch wrote that the name "everlasting Father" designated the Messiah "as the possessor of eternity" who would rule His people like a loving, faithful father.[2] Eternality is exclusively an attribute of God. Thus, through this name, Isaiah 9:6 ascribed eternality and, therefore, deity to the Messiah.

Names in biblical times were designed to reveal the nature of a person. Thus both of these names in Isaiah 9:6 were intended to reveal the divine nature of the Messiah.

In Daniel 7:13 a unique being was brought before the Ancient of days (God). The language implies that this being was a separate person from the Ancient of days.

Ancient Judaism identified this being as the Messiah. The author of the *Similitudes* in the *Book of Enoch* (written during the time between the Old and New Testaments) and other Jewish commentators made this identification.[3]

Daniel 7:13 states that this being "came with the clouds of heaven." The Bible declares that the clouds are the chariot of the LORD God (Ps. 104:1–3) and consistently associates His movements with clouds (Ex. 13:21; 19:9; Isa. 19:1). In light of this association, Daniel 7:13 ascribed deity to the Messiah by describing this being as coming "with the clouds of heaven."

The priests and Sanhedrin of ancient Israel believed that only deity comes with the clouds of heaven. They accused Jesus of blasphemy when He claimed He would come with the clouds of heaven in fulfillment of Daniel 7:13 (Mt. 26:57–66). They recognized that He was claiming deity for Himself.

God's Command to Angels

God commanded all of His angels to worship Jesus Christ (Heb. 1:6). This command is significant for several reasons. Jesus Himself indicated that only deity is to be worshiped (Mt. 4:10). Holy angels rebuked a man who tried to worship them and made it clear that deity is to be the object of worship (Rev. 19:10; 22:8–9). The apostle Paul warned against worshiping angels (Col. 2:18), and both he and the apostle Peter forbade the worship of themselves because they were human beings (Acts 14:8–18; 10:25–26).

These statements indicate that no creatures are to be worshiped—only deity. Thus God's command to the angels to worship Jesus Christ implied He possessed deity.

Humans' Worship

The wise men from the East worshiped Jesus when He was a child (Mt. 2:1–2, 11). As an adult, Jesus was worshiped by a leper (Mt. 8:2), a ruler (Mt. 9:18), His disciples (Mt. 14:33; 28:17), a Gentile woman (Mt. 15:25), two women (Mt. 28:9), a demon-possessed man (Mk. 5:6), and a man whom He had healed of blindness (Jn. 9:38). It appears that all of these people believed Jesus was a divine being.

Jesus accepted this worship. He never rebuked people for worshiping Him. His response is significant in light of the fact that He Himself indicated that only deity is to be worshiped. It implied that He was conscious of His deity.

Jesus' Claim

Jesus claimed deity for Himself in several ways. First, He asserted, "Before Abraham was, I am" (Jn. 8:58). If Jesus had said, "Before Abraham was, I *was*" (past tense), He would have implied that He existed before Abraham came into existence. But Jesus said, "I *am*" (present tense). That statement implied much more than preexistence. Leon Morris wrote, "It is eternity of being and not simply being which lasted through several centuries that the expression indicates."[4]

The Jews were familiar with the expression "I am" and its implication. It was used in their Septuagint version of the Old Testament to express the eternality of God.[5] According to Barrett, the tense of "I am," as used in the Septuagint for God and by Jesus for Himself, "is a properly continuous tense, implying neither beginning nor end of existence." It therefore "(i) indicates the eternal being of Jesus" and "(ii) thereby, and in itself, places Jesus on a level with God."[6] In essence Jesus was saying, "Before Abraham came into being, I eternally was, as now I am, and ever continue to be."[7]

Jesus' hearers recognized He was claiming eternality and, therefore, deity for Himself. Concerning their action recorded in John 8:59, Leon Morris wrote, "The Jews could interpret this as nothing other than blasphemy. Therefore, they took up stones to stone Him, this being the proper punishment for that offence (Lev. 24:16)."[8]

Second, on another occasion Jesus declared, "I and my Father are one" (Jn. 10:30). He did not mean that He and the Father were the same person. The word translated "one" is neuter in gender. It therefore refers to "'one thing' and not 'one person'."[9] Thus God the Father and Jesus Christ were two distinct persons, not two different expressions of the same person.

Jesus' hearers decided to stone Him to death in response to His declaration (Jn. 10:31). This action indicates they understood it. To them it was far more than an assertion of oneness with the Father in purpose and will. It was a declaration of oneness in essence or nature with the Father. Jesus was claiming absolute deity for Himself. They said, "For a good work we stone thee not, but for blasphemy; and because that thou, being a man, makest thyself God" (Jn. 10:33).

Jesus did not tell His hearers that their understanding of His declaration was wrong, implying He agreed with it and, therefore, was claiming deity for Himself.

Third, Jesus claimed to be the Son of God. On one occasion He clearly stated, "I am the Son of God" (Jn. 10:36). More than once His enemies testified He made that claim (Mt. 27:43; Jn. 19:7).

In The Old Testament and writings of postbiblical Judaism, the Hebrew words for "son" were "often used to denote the relationship which determines the nature of a man."[10] It signified that a son has the same nature as his father. Thus when Jesus asserted He was the Son of God, He was signifying that He had the same divine nature as God the Father.

Several times Jesus' enemies tried to kill Him because they understood the implications of His claim to be the Son of God. Once "the Jews sought the more to kill him, because he . . . said also that God was his Father, making himself equal with God" (Jn. 5:18). On another occasion, after Jesus said He was the Son of God, "they sought again to take him; but he escaped out of their hand" (Jn. 10:36, 39). When Jesus was on trial before Pilate, His enemies said, "by our law he ought to die, because he made himself the Son of God" (Jn. 19:7).

OTHER PERSONS

God the Father

God the Father ascribed deity to Jesus. Psalm 45:7 states, "Therefore God, thy God, hath anointed thee." This verse calls two distinct persons "God" (*Elohim*). The term *Elohim* denotes the kind or nature of a being, signifying "what is divine as distinct from what is human."[11] Thus Psalm 45 refers to two distinct divine beings. According to the writer of Hebrews (1:8–9), one of those beings was God the Father addressing His Son, Jesus, with an ascription of deity.

Apostle John

The apostle John ascribed deity to Jesus. Referring to Jesus as "the Word," John wrote, "and the Word was God" (Jn. 1:1). John did not write, "and the Word was *the* God" because that would mean that the Word was

God the Father. John wrote "God" without "the" for a purpose. He wanted to signify that although Jesus, as the Word, was a distinct person from God the Father, He was of the same divine essence or nature as God.[12]

Apostle Paul

The apostle Paul ascribed deity to Jesus. Concerning Jesus, Paul wrote, "In him dwelleth all the fullness of the Godhead bodily" (Col. 2:9). The Greek terms Paul used indicate that deity in its entirety took up permanent residence in the physical human body of Jesus at His incarnation.[13]

Those Who Called Jesus "the Son of God"

I noted earlier that the designation "the Son of God" involved an ascription of deity. Demons (Mt. 8:29), disciples (Mt. 14:33), Roman soldiers (Mt. 27:54), Mark (Mk. 1:1), the angel Gabriel (Lk. 1:35), Satan (Lk. 4:3, 9; the sense of the Greek in his statement is, "Since you are the Son of God"), John the Baptist (Jn. 1:34), Nathanael (Jn. 1:49), Martha (Jn. 11:27), Peter (Mt. 16:16), John (Jn. 20:31), and Paul (Acts 9:20) all called Jesus "the Son of God." They thereby ascribed deity to Him.

CONCLUSION

Any person who rejects the deity of Jesus of Nazareth thereby rejects not only the witness of Jesus but also that of God; the Old Testament; angels; and several human beings, including John the Baptist and apostles. In essence, that person insinuates that all of these witnesses, including God Himself, were in error when they ascribed deity to Jesus. Such an insinuation invites serious consequences.

CHAPTER ELEVEN

JESUS CHRIST'S INCARNATION

Historically some people and groups have denied that Christ became incarnated in human flesh. For example, some said the Christ came temporarily on an already existing man, Jesus of Nazareth. He came long enough to impart a secret body of knowledge to mankind then left the man Jesus before he went to the cross. Thus it was not the Christ who died on the cross. Others claimed the Christ appeared to have a human body; but it was only a nonphysical, phantom appearance. Both views denied that the Christ had a human body and nature of His own.

By contrast, the Scriptures teach that the eternal, preexistent, divine Christ became incarnated in human flesh at a specific time in history. As a result, He had His own human body and human nature.

BIBLICAL EVIDENCES FOR THE INCARNATION

Human Genealogies

Matthew 1:1–17 and Luke 3:23–38 give two different human genealogies for Jesus Christ. Matthew seems to trace His legal genealogy through

His stepfather, Joseph, and thereby presents Christ's legal right to the throne of His ancestor David. It appears that Luke tracks His biological line of descent through His human mother, Mary, and thereby presents His biological right to David's throne.[1] Luke's genealogy demonstrates that Jesus Christ has genuine human ancestors.

Apostle John's Witness

John 1:1, 14. After presenting Christ as the eternal Word, John declared, "And the Word was made flesh, and dwelt among us." The word translated "was made" indicates entrance into a new condition, the act of becoming something a person was not before.[2] The word *flesh* refers to "a human being in contrast to God and other supernatural beings."[3] Thus John said that through incarnation, the eternal Christ became something He was not before—a human being.

The verb translated "dwelt" means "tabernacled."[4] Just as eternal deity tabernacled in a tent among the Israelites in Old Testament times, so the incarnate Jesus Christ was eternal deity tabernacling in human flesh among human beings for more than 30 years.[5]

John 19:18, 28, 33–34, 36, 40–42. John recorded the fact that Jesus Christ had a physical, human body with bones, legs, and blood; was crucified; experienced thirst; was pierced with a spear; and was buried.

1 John 1:1. John used four verbs to declare what he and others had experienced with Christ during His earthly life. The first two express the fact that they had personally "heard" and "seen" Christ in a physical, human body.[6] The perfect tense of these verbs indicates that this experience with the incarnate Christ left a lasting impression on them. "Often seeing and hearing together constitute the totality of sensual and spiritual perception which underlies eyewitness, personal experience, and individual certainty."[7]

John used two other verbs to emphasize that what he and others proclaimed concerning Christ's incarnation was based on more than sight and sound. According to Westcott, the third verb ("have looked upon") "expresses the calm, intent, continuous contemplation of an object which remains before the spectator."[8] Through the fourth verb, "have handled," John signified that he and others had actually felt the physical substance of Christ's body. (See Luke 24:39.) Together these two verbs indicate "definite investigation by the observer."[9]

All four verbs stress the reliability of the eyewitness testimony of John and others that Christ had a physical, human body while on earth.

1 John 4:2–3. John opposed false prophets who, while under the influence of evil spirits, denied the incarnation of Christ in human flesh. He wrote, "every spirit that confesseth that Jesus Christ is come in the flesh is of God; And every spirit that confesseth not that Jesus Christ is come in the flesh is not of God; and this is that spirit of antichrist." John indicated that those who deny Christ's incarnation are influenced by the same evil spirit that will influence the future Antichrist.

Apostle Paul's Witness

1 Corinthians 15:3–4. In his definition of the gospel by which people are saved, Paul included the death, burial, and resurrection of Christ. The fact that Christ experienced physical death, burial in a tomb, and resurrection from the dead clearly indicates He had a physical, human body.

Ephesians 2:13–15. Paul referred to "the blood of Christ" (v. 13) and "his flesh" (v. 15). Using the possessive expressions "of Christ" and "his," Paul indicated that Christ had His own physical, human body. His body was neither a phantom appearance without physical substance nor another man's body that Christ used temporarily.

Philippians 2:7–8. Paul presented three results of the divine Christ's coming into the world. First, He "was made [literally, "became"] in the likeness of men." The word translated "men" refers to human beings, in contrast to animals, plants, angels, and God.[10]

The word translated "likeness" "expresses with great accuracy the Apostle's idea. Christ walked this earth in the *real* likeness of men. This was no mere phantom, no mere incomplete copy of humanity. And yet Paul feels that it did not express the whole of Christ's nature."[11] In other words, although the incarnate Christ was truly a human being, He was also absolute deity. Johannes Schneider expressed it this way: "The divine figure entered history. This is only another way of saying what John says in 1:14: 'The Word was made flesh'."[12]

Second, Paul stated that Christ was "being found in fashion as a man." Johannes Schneider wrote that this phrase "does not merely express the reality of His humanity. There is special stress on the fact that throughout His life, even to the death on the cross, Jesus was in the humanity demonstrated by His earthly form. . . . The reference is to His whole nature and manner as man."[13] In other words, He was truly human, both in nature and conduct. The word translated "being found" indicates that while Christ was on earth, other people recognized His humanity.[14]

Third, Paul signified that Christ died by crucifixion. Spirit beings do not die; thus Paul's statement implied that Christ had a physical, human body.

Colossians 1:21–22. Paul declared that Christ reconciled sinful human beings to God "in the body of his flesh through death." *Body of flesh* was a Hebrew expression for a physical body.[15] Paul used that Hebraism to emphasize that Christ had a physical body that consisted of His own flesh and that experienced physical death.

Everett F. Harrison explained the reason for this emphasis:

There can be no doubt that the language is designed deliberately to counteract the false spiritualism advanced by the error that threatened the church. That false spiritualism maintained that no being possessed of a material body could possibly accomplish reconciliation to a deity who was pure spirit. The angels qualified at this point, and Jesus Christ did not. But the stubborn fact of history had to be emphasized. The Son of God had come in the flesh (Jn. 1:14), had lived His life on earth in the flesh (Heb. 5:7), and in the flesh had offered Himself on the cross as an offering for sin.[16]

Thus Paul was stressing "the necessary bond between" Christ's "incarnation and His atoning death."[17]

1 Timothy 3:16. Paul stated that Christ "was manifest in the flesh." The verb translated "was manifest" means "to become visible," "to be revealed."[18] Thus D. Edmond Hiebert wrote that Paul's words concerning Christ are "a statement of the Incarnation and imply an unveiling of a previous existence."[19] Paul was saying that Christ, who existed from eternity past as a heavenly spirit being, invisible to mortal mankind, became visible to human beings by means of incarnation in human flesh on the earth.

Book of Hebrews' Witness

In Hebrews 2:14–17 the writer made three statements emphasizing Christ's incarnation. First, "forasmuch, then, as the children are partakers of flesh and blood, he also himself likewise took part of the same" (v. 14). The meaning and perfect tense of the verb translated "are partakers" emphasize the common sharing of the same flesh and blood nature by all human beings throughout the history of the human race.[20]

The word translated "likewise" "is used in situations where no differentiation is intended, in the sense *in just the same way.*"[21]

The verb translated "took part" "expresses the unique fact of the Incarnation as a voluntary acceptance of humanity."[22]

Thus, before Christ's incarnation, the flesh and blood nature common to mankind was not part of His eternal being. But "at a fixed point in time, by His own choice, 'he also himself in like manner partook of the same' and so began to share fully the nature of those whom He willed to redeem."[23]

Second, "For verily he took not on him the nature of angels, but he took on him the seed of Abraham" (v. 16). The verbs translated "took on" mean "to bring into one's sphere."[24] Christ did not take into His being the nature of angels. Instead, since God had promised blessing for all mankind through a physical, human descendant of Abraham (Gen. 22:18), Christ took into His being a complete human nature by becoming a physical, human descendant of Abraham in order to help all mankind (Acts 3:25–26; Gal. 3:16).

Third, "Wherefore, in all things it behooved him to be made like his brethren, that he might be a merciful and faithful high priest in things pertaining to God" (v. 17). The word translated "behooved" "speaks of a more inward obligation and necessity incumbent on Christ the high priest."[25] Thus the writer was indicating that "the nature of the work Jesus came to accomplish demanded the Incarnation."[26]

Apostle Peter's Witness

Acts 2:22–24. Peter identified Jesus of Nazareth as "a man" (v. 22). The word he used refers to an adult male human being in contrast to women and children (Mt. 14:21) and pure spirit beings (Acts 14:15; Rom. 1:23).[27]

Peter also declared that Jesus was "crucified and slain" (v. 23). The word translated "crucified" means "fix," "fasten to," or "nail to."[28] Peter used it to describe the nailing of Jesus to the cross.[29] The word translated "slain" refers to "killing by violence, in battle, by execution, murder, or assassination."[30]

Peter asserted that Jesus was resurrected from the dead (v. 24), and he made it clear that this Jesus who was crucified and resurrected from the dead was Christ (vv. 30–32, 36).

Through these statements, Peter clearly indicated that while on earth, Christ was a male human being with a physical body that was nailed to a cross, died, and was resurrected from the dead. He was not just a spirit being.

1 Peter 1:18–19, 21. Peter wrote that sinful human beings were "redeemed . . . with the precious blood of Christ" (vv. 18–19) and God resurrected Christ from the dead (v. 21). These statements signify that Christ had a physical human body that contained blood, died, and was resurrected.

1 Peter 2:24. Peter said that Christ "his own self bore our sins in his own body on the tree . . . by whose stripes ye were healed." Through the possessive pronoun *his* in the expression *his own body*, Peter made it clear that Christ possessed a physical body of His own. It was not the body of another man that was nailed to the cross.

The word translated "stripes" refers to welts, bruises, or wounds caused by blows to a body.[31] Peter thereby signified that Christ had a literal, physical body that suffered welts, bruises, and wounds. He did not have a nonphysical, phantom appearance of a body.

Pilate's Witness

After Pontius Pilate, the Roman procurator, examined Christ, he said to the crowd, "I am innocent of the blood of this righteous person" (Mt. 27:24). He thereby testified that Christ had a physical human body containing blood. When he brought Christ before the crowd, he declared, "Behold the man!" (Jn. 19:5). The word translated "man" refers to human beings in contrast to animals, plants, angels, and God.[32] Thus Pilate declared that Christ was a human being.

Angel Gabriel's Witness

Gabriel told the virgin Mary that she would conceive in her womb and give birth to a son named Jesus (Lk. 1:31). He indicated that that son would be a physical descendant of King David (v. 32). Gabriel's statements explained how the eternal, divine Christ would become incarnated—by conception in and birth through a human mother.

Among the Jews in biblical times, the term *son* was "often used to denote the relationship which determines the nature of a man."[33] In light of this significance, Gabriel's statements implied that as a result of His biological son relationship to a human mother, Jesus Christ would have a complete human nature.

Elisabeth's Witness

When Mary visited her relative, the Holy Spirit supernaturally prompted Elisabeth to say to Mary, "Blessed is the fruit of thy womb" (Lk. 1:42). Norval Geldenhuys explained the significance of Elisabeth's statement as follows: "By these words it is clearly indicated that, although begotten by the Holy Ghost, Jesus, according to His human nature, was really born of the flesh and blood of Mary, and is therefore truly Man."[34]

Elisabeth also called Mary "the mother of my Lord" (v. 43). The combination of the title *mother* and the expression *fruit of thy womb* indicated that Mary was the biological human source of the one born through her; therefore, the one born was also human. By New Testament times, the title *Lord* was commonly used to communicate the idea of absolute deity. Therefore, the fact that the Holy Spirit prompted Elisabeth to call the one born of Mary "my Lord" was significant. It implied that Jesus Christ was more than a human being. He was a divine being incarnated through a human birth.

Birth and Presentation Records

The biblical records of Christ's birth and presentation in the Temple present terms and expressions that signify that Christ became incarnated.

Matthew 1:18 refers to "the birth of Jesus Christ," "his mother, Mary," and the fact that Mary "was found with child." Verse 25 states that she "brought forth her first-born son."

Matthew 2 begins with, "Now when Jesus was born in Bethlehem of Judæa" (v. 1). It records the wise men's question, "Where is he that is born King of the Jews?" (v. 2) and Herod's inquiry concerning "where the Christ should be born" (v. 4). It also relates that the wise men "saw the young child with Mary, his mother" (v. 11).

Luke 2 records that Mary's "days were accomplished that she should be delivered. And she brought forth her first-born son, and wrapped him in swaddling clothes, and laid him in a manger" (vv. 6–7). It presents the angel's proclamation to the shepherds: "Unto you is born this day in the city of David a Savior, who is Christ the Lord. . . . Ye shall find the babe wrapped in swaddling clothes, lying in a manger" (vv. 11–12).

Luke 2 also refers to Christ's conception in Mary's womb and His circumcision (v. 21). Plus it relates that He was brought to Jerusalem to be presented to the Lord because He was a "male that openeth the womb" (vv. 22–23).

A mere phantom or pure spirit being would not have a human birth or mother and would not be a male who opens a womb. In addition, because a phantom or spirit being would not have a physical body, it could not be wrapped in swaddling clothes, laid in a manger, or circumcised.

COMPLETENESS OF THE INCARNATION

If in His incarnation Christ had taken to Himself a human body but not a complete human nature, His incarnation would have been incomplete. He would not have become a total human being. The Bible gives evidences to the effect that His incarnation was complete—that He became a total human being with a complete human nature.

Normal Human Development

Luke wrote that "the child grew" (2:40), meaning Christ experienced normal, human, physical growth.[35]

Luke also stated that "Jesus increased in wisdom and stature" (2:52). The word translated "stature" usually referred to age.[36] Thus, although the eternal Christ possessed all knowledge and wisdom and was ageless in the realm of His deity, He experienced normal human development in wisdom and age in the realm of His humanity.

Subject to Parents

Although in the realm of His deity Jesus was sovereign Lord over His parents, as a child He voluntarily submitted Himself to their paternal authority in the realm of His humanity (Lk. 2:51).

Human Emotions

When He witnessed the sorrow caused by Lazarus' death, Jesus "groaned in the spirit, and was troubled" and "wept" (Jn. 11:33, 35). The word translated "groaned" refers to anger or displeasure that He experienced toward death because of its devastating effects.[37] The word translated "troubled" indicates that He was agitated in mind or spirit.[38] His weeping was prompted by grief.

The night before His crucifixion, Christ experienced "agony" as He prayed earnestly to God the Father (Lk. 22:44). The word for "agony" refers to the inner conflict, tension, or anxiety a person experiences "in face of imminent decisions or disasters."[39]

Human Limitations

Jesus Christ experienced physical hunger for food after fasting for 40 days and nights (Mt. 4:2) and while walking from Bethany to Jerusalem (Mk. 11:12). He had to sleep (Lk. 8:23) and was tired from walking a long distance (Jn. 4:6). He became thirsty while on the cross (Jn. 19:28).

Human Soul and Spirit

Christ talked about His soul being "exceedingly sorrowful" (Mt. 26:38) and "troubled" (Jn. 12:27).

The Scriptures state that He "sighed deeply in his spirit" (Mk. 8:12) and commended His spirit into the Father's hands (Lk. 23:46).

PERMANENCE OF CHRIST'S INCARNATION

The change Christ experienced in the incarnation was permanent. He did not cease being incarnate after He finished His redemptive work. Once He became a human being, He remained a human being and will remain so forever, as indicated by the following facts.

First, Christ still had a physical human body with the wounds of crucifixion after His resurrection. People held Him by the feet after He rose from the dead (Mt. 28:9). In one of His postresurrection appearances, He said, "Behold my hands and my feet, that it is I myself; handle me and see; for a spirit hath not flesh and bones, as ye see me have" (Lk. 24:39).

Second, Christ is a human being as He performs His present mediatorial ministry in heaven. Several years after Christ ascended to heaven, the apostle Paul wrote, "For there is one God, and one mediator between God and men, the man, Christ Jesus" (1 Tim. 2:5). The word translated "man" refers to a human being.[40]

Third, several decades after His ascension to heaven, Christ told the apostle John that He was still "the root and the offspring of David" (Rev. 22:16).

Fourth, Christ signified that He will still be "the Son of man" at His future Second Coming (Mt. 24:30; 26:64).

CONCLUSION

The Bible clearly reveals that through incarnation at a point in time, the eternal, divine Christ became a human being with a physical body and human nature. He was truly human as well as truly divine, the *only* God-Man.

CHAPTER TWELVE

JESUS CHRIST'S HYPOSTATIC UNION

Jesus Christ is both deity and humanity in essence. The incarnated Christ has a complete divine nature and a complete human nature inseparably united in one person. Thus He is a theanthropic person, a God-Man.

The word *theanthropic* is derived from the combination of two Greek words: *theos (God)* and *anthropos (man)*. Theologians call this union of two complete natures in Jesus Christ "the hypostatic union" because it is the real essence of the incarnated Christ.

The English word *hypostasis* is derived from a Greek word meaning "essence, actual being, reality."[1] Thus it refers to the real essence of a person or thing. As applied to Christ, it is related to the issue of the real essence of the incarnated Jesus Christ.

Meaning of Nature

The term *nature,* when used in such expressions as "divine nature" and "human nature," refers to a unique combination of attributes that determines the kind of a being or thing. A divine nature is a unique combination of attributes that makes a being divine instead of an angel, an animal, a plant, or a human being. A human nature is a unique combination of attributes that makes a being a human being instead of an angel, an animal, a plant, or a divine being.

Because a nature determines the kind of being, the union of a complete divine nature and a complete human nature in the incarnated Christ makes Him a God-Man kind of being. No other being possessed the union of these two natures prior to Christ's incarnation, and no other being will possess it in the future. The incarnated Jesus Christ is the only God-Man and, therefore, is a unique being.

BIBLICAL REVELATION OF CHRIST'S HYPOSTATIC UNION

At least two Old Testament passages foretold that the Messiah would be a God-Man, with deity and humanity united in the same person.

Isaiah 9:6–7

By God's revelation, the prophet Isaiah presented several names for the Messiah. According to Edward J. Young, those names "are accurate descriptions and designations of His being. In the Bible the name indicates the character, essence or nature of a person or object."[2] In an earlier chapter, we saw that two of those names ("Mighty God" (el gibbor) and "Everlasting Father") ascribed deity to the Messiah.

In addition, Isaiah declared that the Messiah would be a child who was born. Because deity is not born but humanity is, this declaration indicated that the Messiah would also be a human being.

Thus, according to Isaiah's prophecy, the Messiah would possess the union of deity and humanity. In light of this, Young wrote concerning Isaiah: "By means of the words yeled, 'child,' and yullad, 'is born,' he has called attention to the Messiah's humanity, but by the phrase 'el gibbor' we are brought face to face with Messiah's deity."[3] In essence, Isaiah foretold that the Messiah would be a God-Man and, therefore, a unique being.

Another name that Isaiah indicated would apply to the Messiah— "Wonderful" (literally, "Wonder")—emphasized His uniqueness. Concerning the name "Wonder," Young stated, "In reality this is stronger than if he had used an adjective. Not merely is the Messiah wonderful but He is Himself a Wonder, through and through."[4] Indeed, the fact that the

Messiah would possess a union of complete deity and complete humanity as His real essence would make Him a wonder. What mere human being can fully comprehend the uniqueness of this person?

Daniel 7:13

In this part of a revelational vision that God gave to the prophet Daniel, the Messiah was portrayed as being "like the Son of man" (literally, "like a son of man" in the Aramaic text) and coming "with the clouds of heaven." The expression *a son of man* indicated that the Messiah would be human, an offspring of mankind; but the word *like* implied that He would be more than human. Several Old Testament passages signified that the clouds are God's chariot (Ps. 104:3; Isa. 19:1). Thus the fact that this divinely revealed vision portrayed the Messiah as coming "with the clouds of heaven" indicated He would also be deity. Daniel was seeing a person who would be deity incarnated in humanity.

Gleason L. Archer, Jr., wrote concerning this prophetic portrayal of the Messiah,

The personage who now appears before God in the form of a human being is of heavenly origin. He has come to this place of coronation accompanied by the clouds of heaven and is clearly no mere human being in essence. The expression "like a son of man" (kebar 'enas) identifies the appearance of this final Ruler of the world not only as a man, in contrast to the beasts (the four world empires), but also as the heavenly Sovereign incarnate.[5]

At least three New Testament passages signified that Jesus Christ fulfilled the Isaiah 9:6–7 and Daniel 7:13 prophecies foretelling that the Messiah would be a God-Man.

John 1:1, 14

When referring to Jesus Christ as "the Word," the apostle John wrote, "and the Word was God" (Jn. 1:1). He did not write, "and the Word was *the* God," because that would mean the Word was God the Father. John wrote the word *God* without *the* for a purpose. He wanted to signify that, although Jesus as the Word was a distinct person from God the Father, He was of the same divine essence or nature as God.[6]

After presenting Jesus Christ's deity in verse 1, John declared, "And the Word was made flesh, and dwelt among us" (Jn. 1:14). The word translated "was made" indicates entrance into a new condition, the act of becoming something a person was not before.[7] The word *flesh* refers to "a *human being in contrast to God and other supernatural beings.*"[8] Thus John said that through incarnation the divine Christ became something that He was not before; He became a human being.

The verb translated "dwelt" means "tabernacled."[9] Just as eternal deity tabernacled in a tent among the Israelites in Old Testament times, so the incarnate Jesus Christ was eternal deity tabernacling in human flesh among human beings for more than 30 years.[10]

Romans 1:3–4

In Romans 1:3 the apostle Paul referred to God's "Son, Jesus Christ our Lord"; and in verse 4 he called Jesus "the Son of God." In the Old Testament and writings of postbiblical Judaism, the Hebrew words for "son" were "often used to denote the relationship which determines the nature of a man."[11] Thus, by applying the title "the Son of God" to Jesus Christ, Paul signified that He had the same divine nature as God the Father.

Paul further stated that God's Son "was made of the seed of David according to the flesh" (v. 3). God's Son became a physical, human descendant of King David. Concerning the expression *according to the flesh*, John Murray wrote, "In the usage of the New Testament, when applied to Christ, the denotation cannot be other than human nature in its entirety."[12] Thus Paul's statement indicated that Jesus Christ was God's divine Son who assumed complete humanity and thereby became a God-Man.

Galatians 4:4

The apostle Paul wrote, "But, when the fullness of the time was come, God sent forth his Son, made of a woman." The opening part of this statement signifies that Paul was referring to an event that took place at a point of time in history. That event was God's sending forth His Son from heaven to earth. The words *sent forth* imply that the Son already existed in heaven before He was sent.[13] The designation *his Son* signifies that the one whom God sent possessed complete deity.

The fact that, in His being sent by God, the Son was "made [literally, "from," not "of" or "through"] a woman" indicates that "the woman was not only the medium of His coming into the flesh, but from her He took all that belongs to the human."[14] Thus Paul asserted that at a point of time in history, God sent His completely divine, preexisting Son from heaven to earth to assume complete humanity and thereby become a God-Man.

RELATIONSHIP OF CHRIST'S TWO NATURES IN THE HYPOSTATIC UNION

First, the two natures are united without loss of separate identity. Christ's human nature always remains human, and His divine nature always remains divine. There is no mixture of the attributes of one nature with those of the other. A mixture would cause the human nature to cease being a human nature, the divine nature to cease being a divine nature, and Christ to cease being fully God and fully Man. A mixture would change the real essence of the incarnated Christ.

Second, the two natures are united without either losing any of its attributes. When Christ became incarnated, His divine nature did not lose any of its attributes, and He did not take to Himself only a partial human nature. His divine nature remained a complete divine nature, and He took to Himself a complete human nature. Thus He is fully God and fully Man. If either nature were minus any of its attributes, Christ's essence would be different than it is.

Third, although Christ has two complete natures, He remains one person. He is not two persons. The attributes of both natures belong to His person. While on earth Christ performed some functions in the realm of His humanity (i.e., walked from place to place, Jn. 4:3–6) and others in the realm of His deity (i.e., held the whole universe together, Col. 1:17), but in both instances one person was acting. Thus, at the same time, this one person could be physically tired and omnipotent, growing in wisdom and omniscient, finite and infinite, limited to one location and omnipresent.

IMPORTANCE OF CHRIST'S HYPOSTATIC UNION

The hypostatic union of the incarnated Jesus Christ is important for at least two reasons.

First, it was necessary for Christ to be the perfect revealer of God to mankind. Only deity can perfectly reveal deity, but Christ also had to be human to give that revelation in a manner human beings could grasp (Jn. 1:18; 14:7–9; Col. 1:15; Heb. 1:3).

Second, it was necessary for the work of redemption. The Redeemer had to be one person who was both human and divine. He had to be human both to die and to die as mankind's substitute. He also had to be divine for two reasons: so that He could die for all human beings and so that His death might have infinite value (1 Tim. 2:5–6; Heb. 2:14–17).

CONCLUSION

When Jesus Christ, the Son of God, came to earth and became a man to show us what the Father is like and to provide salvation for our sins through His death on the cross, he did not give up his divine nature. Instead, that nature was joined to a human nature. Thus He has two complete natures and is the only true God-Man.

CHAPTER THIRTEEN

JESUS CHRIST'S KENOSIS

When Jesus Christ came to earth to be incarnated, He "made himself of no reputation" (Phil. 2:7), according to the apostle Paul. The verb translated "made of no reputation" is *ekenosen*. Theologians have used the major part of that verb to form the term *kenosis*. As a result, *kenosis* has become the theological term for Jesus Christ's action that Paul described in Philippians 2:6–8.

The verb Paul used means "to empty."[1] Thus, in Philippians 2:7, Paul stated that Christ emptied Himself of something. That emptying activity was the kenosis of Christ.

Relationship of Christ's Kenosis to His Incarnation

Paul presented two concepts that indicate a relationship between Christ's kenosis and His incarnation. First, he stated that Christ emptied Himself "and was made in the likeness of men" (v. 7). Johannes Schneider claimed the expression *was made in the likeness of men* was Paul's way of saying the same thing that the apostle John asserted concerning Christ's incarnation in John 1:14: "the Word was made flesh."[2] Thus Paul indicated that Christ emptied Himself of something in conjunction with His incarnation in human flesh.

Second, Paul also associated Christ's kenosis with His "being found in fashion as a man" (vv. 7–8). Concerning this expression, Schneider wrote, "There is special stress on the fact that throughout His life, even to the death on the cross, Jesus was in the humanity demonstrated by His earthly form. . . . The reference is to His whole nature and manner as man."[3] Schneider also asserted that the word translated "being found" indicates that throughout Jesus' earthly life, His humanity "could be seen by anybody."[4] Thus, through this second expression, Paul again signified that Christ emptied Himself of something in conjunction with His becoming a human being through His incarnation.

An Important Question

In light of what Paul wrote, an important question must be asked. Of what did Christ empty Himself in conjunction with His incarnation? Several answers have been proposed, giving birth to different views concerning the kenosis of Jesus Christ.

Incorrect Views of the Kenosis

There are at least two incorrect views of Christ's kenosis. One view asserts that Christ emptied Himself of *all* of His divine attributes or deity when He became incarnated.

The other view claims that, when Christ became incarnated, He emptied Himself of *some* of His divine attributes or deity, especially the attributes of omniscience, omnipotence, and omnipresence. Advocates of this view argue that because Jesus Christ grew in wisdom as a child (Lk. 2:52), He must not have been omniscient (all-knowing). Because He experienced physical weariness and could be beaten, scourged, and crucified by human beings, He must not have been omnipotent (all-powerful). Because He resorted to walking or taking a boat to get from one location to another, He must not have been omnipresent (everywhere present at the same time).

There are at least two major problems with both of these views. First, both contradict Paul's statement that in Christ "dwelleth all the fullness of the Godhead bodily" (Col. 2:9). Curtis Vaughan wrote that the Greek terms Paul used in this statement indicate that deity in its entirety took up permanent residence in the physical body of Jesus Christ at His incarnation.[5] Reinier Schippers stated that Paul's terms "must mean deity, Godhead, entirety, the sum total of divine attributes."[6] Thus Paul emphasized that the physical body of the incarnated Christ housed deity in its totality. No divine attribute was missing.

Second, as noted in the previous chapter, a divine nature or a human nature is a unique combination of attributes that determines the kind of a being or thing. Thus a divine nature is a unique combination of attributes that makes a being deity instead of an angel, animal, plant, or human. Because this is so, the loss of even one of that nature's attributes would destroy its unique combination and thereby cause it to cease being a divine nature. The loss of any attribute would change it into a different kind of nature.

In light of this fact, if Christ emptied Himself of even one attribute of His divine nature in His incarnation, then His divine nature ceased being a divine nature and Christ ceased being absolute deity. Thus both of these incorrect views of Christ's kenosis are destructive of the deity of the incarnate Christ.

Correct View of the Kenosis

The correct view of the kenosis is based on Paul's contrast between "the form of God" and "the form of a servant" (literally, "of a slave," Phil. 2:6–7). Paul implied that Christ exchanged the form of God for the form of a slave in conjunction with His incarnation. Thus Christ emptied Himself of the form of God.

But what does the "form of God" mean? The word translated "form" refers to "outward appearance."[7] In light of this, His form of God "is the garment by which His divine nature may be known."[8] Thus, in conjunction with His incarnation, Christ emptied Himself not of His deity, but of the outward appearance of His deity.

To appreciate the significance of Christ's emptying Himself of the outward appearance of His deity, we must note several things. First, Paul indicated that before Christ's incarnation, He was equal with God the Father (v. 6). Gustav Stahlin stated that the word translated "equal" signifies an "equality of dignity, will and nature . . . which is both essential and perfect."[9] He further wrote that "Christ was and is equal to God by nature. This equality is a possession which He can neither renounce nor lose."[10]

Second, because Christ was equal with God the Father in dignity and nature, He possessed the same fullness of deity as the Father. As a result, the outward appearance of His deity was as fully visible in the spirit realm as was the Father's outward appearance. This outward appearance was "the image of sovereign divine majesty" and was "visibly expressed in the radiance of heavenly light."[11] That heavenly light was the Shekinah glory of God.

Third, because Christ's outward appearance of His deity was as fully visible as the Father's, special privileges were made available to Him—privileges He could have used for His own advantage and personal benefit.

Fourth, Paul stated that Christ "thought it not robbery to be equal with God" (v. 6). The word translated "thought" means "consider."[12] This meaning, together with the meaning of the word translated "robbery," indicates that Paul taught the following: In His preincarnate existence, Christ did not consider His equality with God, with its outward appearance of deity and available special privileges, as something to be used for His own advantage and personal benefit.[13]

Evidence that Christ did not use His equality with God for His own advantage and personal benefit is seen in the fact that when it was time for Him to enter the world through incarnation, He emptied Himself of the outward appearance of His deity. This emptying involved two things for Him while He was in the world.

First, He veiled His divine glory. (See Isaiah 53:2.) Christ displayed His divine glory only once while on earth in human flesh—when He was transfigured before Peter, James, and John (Mt. 17:1–4; event John referred to in John 1:14).

Second, He did not use His divine attributes to benefit Himself. He did not use them to make His human life easier. He voluntarily submitted to the limitations common to humanity. Although He was omniscient, omnipresent, and omnipotent in His deity, He allowed His humanity to grow in wisdom, kept His body in one place at a time, took time to walk from place to place, and allowed humans to arrest and crucify Him. Thus He greatly restricted the use and manifestation of His divine attributes.

The Great Exchange

When Christ became incarnated, He not only emptied Himself of His form of deity, He also took on Himself "the form of a servant" (Phil. 2:7). The word translated "servant" refers to a slave, a person who must obey the will of another.[14] Thus Christ exchanged the outward appearance of His "sovereign divine majesty" for the outward appearance of an obedient, submissive slave.[15] (See also 2 Corinthians 8:9.)

Christ took on this outward appearance of a slave by humbly submitting in obedience to God's will in two respects: First, He died as a substitutionary sacrifice for the sins of the world in fulfillment of Isaiah 53;[16] and, second, He died on a cross.

It was Christ's death on a cross that especially gave Him the outward appearance of a slave. So many slaves were crucified in the Roman Empire that crucifixion was called the "slaves' punishment."[17] In light of this fact, people of Christ's day would have classified Him with slaves because He died on a cross.

CONCLUSION: THE SUPREME EXAMPLE

What motivated Christ to exchange the outward appearance of His sovereign divine majesty for the outward appearance of an obedient, submissive slave? The answer is love. He was more concerned for the welfare of others than for His own welfare. He gave the supreme example of self-sacrificing love for the benefit of others. Thus in other passages, Paul wrote that Christ "gave himself for our sins" (Gal. 1:4), "loved me and gave himself for me" (Gal. 2:20), and "gave himself for us" (Ti. 2:14).

Paul clearly indicated that Christians are to follow Christ's example. He commanded us to have Christ's mindset of self-sacrificing love for the benefit of others. In Philippians 2:3–5, he wrote, "Let nothing be done through strife or vainglory, but in lowliness of mind let each esteem others better than themselves. Look not every man on his own things, but every man also on the things of others. Let this mind be in you, which was also in Christ Jesus." According to Georg Bertram, Paul was indicating that Christ's mindset in conjunction with His *kenosis* "is itself the standard for the mind of believers whose fellowship is constituted by Christ."[18] Paul again signified the same when he wrote, "And walk in love, as Christ also hath loved us, and hath given himself for us an offering and a sacrifice to God for a sweet-smelling savor" (Eph. 5:2).

CHAPTER FOURTEEN

JESUS CHRIST'S SINLESSNESS

We all struggle with sin—and will continue to do so until we are glorified. Only one man, Jesus Christ, has always been completely sinless. Sinlessness is one of His attributes, or characteristics.

The Meaning of Sinlessness

To establish the meaning of sinlessness, we must first understand the concept of sin. Sin may be defined as "any failure to conform perfectly to the holy character and will of God." God requires people to be holy because He is holy (Lev. 11:44; 1 Pet. 1:15–16), but people fail to fulfill that requirement (Rom. 3:23).

Human sin consists of four basic elements. First is a disposition of enmity against God, often called the sin nature. The Bible teaches that sin is inscribed indelibly on the human heart, the inner control center of humans where all life decisions are made (Jer. 17:1). Therefore, the human heart is "deceitful" and "wicked" (Jer. 17:9) and the source of wrong thoughts and acts (Mt. 15:19). It further declares that "the carnal mind is enmity against God" (Rom. 8:7).

Second, sin involves wrong acts. The Bible classifies such acts as murder, adultery, fornication, theft, false witness, and blasphemy as evil deeds (Mt. 15:19; Jn. 3:19).

Third, sin includes wrong thoughts, attitudes, intents, and impulses. For example, Scripture indicates that lusting after forbidden things and certain kinds of anger are sin (Mt. 5:21–22, 27–28).

Fourth, failure to do good deeds that should be done is sin (1 Sam. 12:23; Jas. 4:17).

On the basis of these facts concerning sin, we can conclude that a sinless person is one who never fails to be conformed perfectly to God's holy character and will. Such a person does not possess a disposition of enmity against God (a sin nature); never commits a wrong act; never has a wrong thought, attitude, intent, or impulse; and never fails to do good deeds that should be done.

Biblical Evidences for Christ's Sinlessness

The Bible provides several lines of evidence for the complete sinlessness of Jesus Christ. First, as a prophet, King David foretold that the Messiah would be God's "Holy One" (Ps. 16:10). Approximately 1,000 years later, the apostles Peter and Paul indicated that, in this prophecy, David was speaking of Jesus Christ (Acts 2:25–32; 13:34–37).

The angel Gabriel declared that the child who would be born of the virgin Mary would be "holy" (Lk. 1:35).

A significant aspect of holiness is the absence of sin. Thus David and Gabriel foretold the sinlessness of Christ.

Second, Jesus Christ claimed He was sinless. To His opponents He threw out the challenge, "Which of you convicteth me of sin?" (Jn. 8:46). Leon Morris called this challenge "a staggering assertion of sinlessness."[1] Merrill C. Tenney claimed Jesus was challenging His opponents to prove Him guilty of sin and that such a challenge "would have been impossible for anyone else to utter. No human being could risk making that challenge without many flaws in his character being made known. . . . Had Jesus not been sinless, someone in the hostile crowd would eagerly have charged him with at least one sin."[2]

Just as "God is light, and in him is no darkness at all" (1 Jn. 1:5), so Christ asserted that He was "the light of the world" in the midst of moral and spiritual darkness (Jn. 8:12; 9:5; 12:35–36). He also signified that because He radiated the light of sinless moral perfection, He would be hated and rejected by sinful human beings (Jn. 3:19–20; 15:22–24).

Third, other people indicated that Jesus Christ was sinless. The apostle John called Jesus "the true Light," lighting people in the midst of moral and spiritual darkness (Jn. 1:4–5, 9).

John also wrote concerning Christ, "in him is no sin" (1 Jn. 3:5). Gustav Stahlin declared that here the word *sin* refers to the characteristic that determines "human nature in hostility to God."[3] David Smith indicated that it denotes "the sinful principle" inside of people that manifests itself outwardly "in specific acts."[4] Thus John said that Jesus did not have inside of Him the disposition of enmity against God (the sin nature).

The apostle Peter declared that Jesus "did no sin" (1 Pet. 2:22). Here the word *sin* refers to "an individual act of sin."[5] Thus Peter said that Christ never committed an act of sin.

Peter also stated that Christ was like "a lamb without blemish and without spot" (1 Pet. 1:19). According to Friedrich Hauck, the word translated "without blemish" denotes "one who is without reproach."[6] Hauck further stated, "The OT demand that sacrifices be without physical blemish finds its NT fulfillment in the perfect moral blamelessness (Heb. 4:15; 7:26) of the Redeemer who sacrifices Himself."[7] Concerning the word translated "without spot," Albrecht Oepke wrote that it presents "the thought of the sinlessness of Jesus."[8]

Paul asserted that Christ "knew no sin" (2 Cor. 5:21). Surely Christ had an intellectual knowledge of the existence and nature of sin as a result of observing human life while He was on earth. So Paul could not have meant that He lacked that knowledge of sin. In light of this fact, we are forced to conclude that Paul meant Christ did not know sin in the sense of having experienced it through personal practice. Thus Murray J. Harris wrote that Christ "was without any acquaintance with sin that might have come through his ever having a sinful attitude or doing a sinful act. Both inwardly and outwardly he was impeccable."[9]

The writer of the book of Hebrews stated that Christ "was in all points tempted like as we are, yet without sin" (Heb. 4:15). Heinrich Seesemann pointed out that "the content of temptation is the seduction into disobedience"; it places a person "in a situation of open choice between surrender to God's will and revolt against it."[10] The writer of Hebrews said that Christ remained sinless throughout His life on earth. His sinlessness was demonstrated by the fact that He "gained victory after victory in the constant battle with temptation that life in this world entails."[11] He persisted "without any weakening of His faith in God or any relaxation of His obedience to Him."[12]

Surely the strongest forms of temptation for Christ were Satan's attempts "in every possible way to deflect Jesus from obedience to God . . . and therewith to render His mission impossible."[13] (See Luke 4:1–13.) No doubt Satan's last and most intense attack with temptation took place within the last hours leading to Christ's death. Merrill C. Tenney wrote, "There could scarcely have been a more favorable moment for pressure than when Jesus was confronted with the final issue of his life."[14]

Jesus knew He would be subjected to a tremendous onslaught from Satan, for on the night before His crucifixion He said, "the prince of this world cometh" (Jn. 14:30). But He continued, "[Satan] hath nothing in me." Tenney asserted that Jesus thereby denoted that "Satan had no claim on him. There was nothing in Jesus' character or action that could be used against him. Satan had no valid accusation that could be used as leverage to divert Jesus from the will of his Father. His obedience had been perfect, and he intended to complete the Father's purpose irrespective of what it might cost him."[15]

The writer of Hebrews also declared that Jesus Christ, as high priest, is "holy, harmless, undefiled, separate from sinners" (Heb. 7:26). The word translated "holy" refers to a person committed to obedience to God and His requirements.[16] The word translated "harmless" signifies "one who has done no evil."[17] The word translated "undefiled" describes a person who is not defiled by inner apostasy that prompts one to treat God's requirements with contempt and to get involved with the pollutions of the world contrary to God's holy will.[18]

Even as the Levitical high priest was required to separate himself from all ritual defilement for seven days before the Day of Atonement, so Jesus was permanently (perfect tense) "separate from sinners" throughout His life before He made the perfect atonement for sin through His sacrificial death.[19] "Although He came to earth 'in the likeness of sinful flesh,' lived among sinners, received sinners, ate with sinners, was known as the friend of sinners," yet He was separate from sinners in the sense that He Himself never sinned.[20]

These descriptions of Christ in Hebrews 7:26 indicate that "in mind and conduct He perfectly fulfils the divine requirements" to be mankind's "perfect High-priest. . . . Hence, as one who is wholly free from sin, He does not need to bring an atoning offering for Himself, like the imperfect priests of the OT."[21] Although Jesus frequently went to the Temple, there is no record of His ever bringing a sin offering for Himself.

One of the thieves who was crucified with Jesus declared that He had "done nothing amiss" (Lk. 23:41). He thereby asserted that Jesus had done nothing "morally *evil, wrong, improper.*"[22]

Jesus Christ was described as being "righteous" or "just" by Pilate, the Roman procurator of Judea (Mt. 27:24); Pilate's wife (Mt. 27:19); a Roman centurion who observed His crucifixion and related events (Lk. 23:47); the apostle Peter (Acts 3:14; 1 Pet. 3:18); Stephen (Acts 7:52); Ananias (Acts 22:12–14); and the apostle John (1 Jn. 2:1, 29; 3:7). In all of these passages, the same word, *dikaios,* is translated "righteous" or "just."

When Pilate, his wife, and the Roman centurion applied this word to Jesus, they probably meant He was innocent of breaking any governmental laws or societal norms and was a moral person.[23] When Peter, Stephen, Ananias, and John ascribed this term to Jesus, they were describing "His total orientation to the will of Him who sent Him."[24] To them, "the righteous Christ is the Doer of the will of God in the fullest sense."[25]

This ascription of righteousness to Jesus Christ corresponded to the ascription of righteousness to the Messiah in the Old Testament.[26] In the Old Testament, "the Messiah is called righteous because His whole nature and action are in conformity with the norm of the divine will."[27] (See Isaiah 11:4–5; 53:11; Jeremiah 23:5–6; and Zechariah 9:9.)

PROBLEMS WITH SINLESSNESS

The Bible clearly teaches that Jesus Christ was totally sinless, but that truth prompts three problem issues that must be explored.

Human Sin Nature

Background. The first issue results from the combination of two truths. First, the Bible teaches that each human being, who has been procreated through natural means since the fall of mankind, is in a state of sin with a sin nature from the moment of conception in the mother. David stated, "I was shaped in iniquity, and in sin did my mother conceive me" (Ps. 51:5; cf. Ps. 58:3; Isa. 48:8). Concerning these statements, Franz Delitzsch wrote,

David here confesses his hereditary sin as the root of his actual sin . . . the meaning is merely, that his parents were sinful human beings, and that this sinful state has operated upon his birth and even his conception, and from this point has passed over to him. . . . That man from his first beginning onwards . . . is tainted with sin; that the proneness to sin with its guilt and corruption is propagated from parents to their children.[28]

In other words, a human being's sin nature is passed on at the moment of conception through the ancestral line of biological descent.

Second, the Bible also teaches that Jesus Christ, in the realm of His humanity, is a biological descendant of human ancestors as the result of His conception in the womb of His mother Mary. At least two things clearly signify Jesus' biological heritage.

The Bible indicates that Jesus Christ is a biological descendant of Abraham. God made the following promise to Abraham: "In thy seed shall all the nations of the earth be blessed" (Gen. 22:18). The Hebrew word translated "seed," when applied to human beings, refers to "human, male 'seed,' 'semen': Lev. 15:16; 22:4; Num. 5:13, 28," and also to "offspring" or "descendants."[29] Thus God promised He would bless all mankind through Abraham's biological line of descent.

Walter C. Kaiser wrote that the word translated "seed" signifies "the whole line of descendants as a unit" but is "flexible enough" to refer to "one person who epitomizes the whole group."[30] In line with this flexibility, the apostle Peter implied that Jesus Christ is the ultimate "seed" of Abraham through whom the promise of Genesis 22:18 is fulfilled (Acts 3:25–26).[31] And the apostle Paul indicated that Jesus Christ is Abraham's ultimate "seed" (Gal. 3:16, 19). Since God had promised to bring blessing for all mankind through Abraham's biological line of descent, the writer of Hebrews asserted that, when Christ became incarnated in order to help human beings, "he took on him the seed of Abraham" (Heb. 2:14–16).

The Greek word translated "seed" in these New Testament statements has the same meanings as the Hebrew word for "seed" in Genesis 22:18, when applied to human beings: "the male seed or semen" and "descendants."[32] In light of this fact, these statements imply that before it was begotten, the humanity of Jesus Christ existed in seminal form in Abraham's body (cf. Heb. 7:5, 9–10) and, therefore, Jesus Christ is a biological descendant of Abraham.

Furthermore, the Bible also indicates that Jesus Christ is a biological descendant of King David. God promised David that his house, kingdom, and throne would be established forever (2 Sam. 7:16). The Hebrew word for "house" in this promise signified a family. "If the ancestor after whom the house was named was a king," then the word referred to a dynasty.[33] Thus God promised that David's family dynasty would be established forever. Since a dynasty is "a sequence of rulers from the same family,"[34] this promise was God's guarantee that there would always be a biological descendant of David available to exercise his ruling authority.

God clearly indicated this fact through three other declarations. First, "My covenant will I not break, nor will I alter the thing that is gone out of my lips. Once have I sworn by my holiness that I will not lie unto David. His seed shall endure forever, and his throne as the sun before me. It shall be established forever like the moon, and as a faithful witness in heaven" (Ps. 89:34–37; see also vv. 3–4, 28–29). Here the Hebrew word for "seed" is the same as that noted earlier in God's Genesis 22:18 promise to Abraham; therefore, God guaranteed that David's biological line of descent would endure forever to exercise his ruling authority.

Second, God promised David, "There shall not fail thee a man in my sight to sit on the throne of Israel" (1 Ki. 8:25; see Jer. 33:17).

Third, "The Lord hath sworn in truth unto David; he will not turn from it: Of the fruit of thy body will I set upon thy throne" (Ps. 132:11). The basic meaning of the Hebrew word translated "body" "seems to be 'inside' (a body or object)."[35] In some passages it refers to "the male procreative organs" (Job 19:17; Mic. 6:7), and in such passages the expression *the fruit of the body* refers to the offspring that a man begets from inside his body.[36] That is the meaning of the expression in Psalm 132:11.[37] God was promising that it would be biological descendants of David, who existed in seminal form in his body, whom He would set on David's throne.

In the Old Testament God foretold that He would set a righteous biological descendant of David on his throne forever (Isa. 9:6–7; 11:1–12; Jer. 23:5–6; 33:15–17; Dan. 7:13–14).

The Jews recognized that these prophecies referred to the Messiah, who would be a biological descendant of David and would abide forever. Some asked, "Hath not the scripture said that Christ cometh of the seed of David . . . ?" (Jn. 7:42). The word for "seed" signifies that they understood that "the Christ promised by the OT will be the 'descendant of David'."[38] Others said, "We have heard out of the law that Christ abideth forever" (Jn. 12:34).

The apostles also recognized that these prophetic passages referred to the Messiah, and they were convinced Jesus Christ was the biological descendant of David who would fulfill these Messianic prophecies.

Peter indicated that Jesus Christ obtained His humanity through biological descent from David. After referring to Psalm 132:11, where God swore with an oath to David "that of the fruit of his loins, according to the flesh, he would raise up Christ to sit on his throne," Peter then said, "This Jesus hath God raised up" (Acts 2:30, 32). The Greek terms translated "the fruit of his loins" express the meaning "one of his descendants."[39]

After referring to David, Paul said, "Of this man's seed hath God, according to his promise, raised unto Israel a Savior, Jesus" (Acts 13:23). The preposition translated "of" denotes a source of something.[40] Paul was claiming that a source of Jesus' humanity was David's biological line of descent.

In Romans 1:3 Paul wrote, "Jesus Christ our Lord . . . was made of the seed of David according to the flesh." The preposition in the expression *of the seed* means "from within."[41] The verb translated "was made" means "come to be."[42] The word translated "flesh" refers to "a human being."[43] Paul claimed that Jesus Christ's humanity came into existence from within David's biological line of descent.

Paul also asserted the same concept when he referred to "Jesus Christ, of the seed of David" (2 Tim. 2:8). Here again he used the preposition that means "from within."

The angel Gabriel indicated that Jesus Christ would be the biological descendant of David who would fulfill the Messianic prophecies of the Old Testament. Concerning Him he said, "The Lord God shall give unto him the throne of his father, David" (Lk. 1:32). Gabriel's terminology identified David as an ancestor of Jesus.

J. A. Motyer related a twofold significance for this ancestry. First, "an unequivocally human ancestry secures the reality of the unequivocal humanity of Jesus." Second, "the reality of the descent of Jesus from David makes him the repository of the promises vouchsafed to but never secured by his famous ancestor."[44]

Jesus Christ identified Himself as "the offspring of David" (Rev. 22:16). The word translated "offspring" refers to a descendant of an ancestor.[45]

126

Jesus claimed to be the fulfillment of Isaiah 11:1, which foretold that the Messiah would be a descendant of David, Jesse's son.[46]

Statement and Proposed Solutions. The combination of the two truths we have observed prompts the following issue: Since a human being's sin nature is passed on at the moment of conception through the ancestral line of biological descent and, since Jesus Christ in the realm of His humanity is a biological descendant of human ancestors as the result of conception in His mother Mary, how could He have been conceived without a sin nature?

In response to this question, it is important to note that Jesus Christ was born of a virgin. His humanity was conceived without a human father. "Like every mother, Mary provided the 23 chromosomes in her ovum," but the Holy Spirit supernaturally prepared and supplied the other 23 chromosomes necessary for the conception of a human being (Lk. 1:30–35).[47]

The fact that His human mother provided half of His human chromosomes but the other half was supplied without a human father may indicate that the sin nature is passed on to human offspring through the father, not the mother. This supposition would be in harmony with the biblical teaching that, in spite of the fact that both Adam and Eve committed the original sin of the human race, mankind fell and became sinful exclusively in Adam, not Adam and Eve (Gen. 3:6; Rom. 5:12–19; 1 Cor. 15:22). In this way Jesus could have been a biological descendant of Abraham, David, and Mary without possessing a sin nature.

If the sin nature is passed on to human offspring through the father and the mother, then it must be concluded that the Holy Spirit supernaturally prevented Mary's sin nature from being passed on to the humanity of Jesus when He caused conception to take place in her. The fact that Mary called God "my Savior" indicates she recognized that she was a sinful human being, possessing a sin nature, and was the recipient of God's gift of salvation (Lk. 1:46–47). Through such prevention by the Holy Spirit, Jesus could have had biological human ancestors without possessing a sin nature.

Sinful Flesh

If it be true that Jesus Christ was sinless, what is meant by the apostle Paul's statement that God sent "his own Son, in the likeness of sinful flesh" (Rom. 8:3)?

The word translated "flesh" refers to *"a human being* in contrast to God and other supernatural beings."[48] In light of this definition, the wording of Paul's statement is crucial. He did *not* say that God sent His Son "in the likeness of flesh" because some might understand that phrase to mean Jesus Christ was similar to human beings but was not truly human. That interpretation would deny the incarnated Christ's humanity and thereby contradict what Paul and other writers of the New Testament taught. (See Colossians 1:21–22 and 1 John 4:2-3.)[49]

In addition, he did *not* say that God sent His Son "in sinful flesh" because that would mean Christ became sinful through His incarnation. "That would have contradicted the sinlessness of Jesus for which the New Testament is jealous throughout."[50]

Instead, Paul *did* say that God sent His Son "in the *likeness* of sinful flesh" (italics added). William F. Arndt and F. Wilbur Gingrich explained the significance of the word translated "likeness" as follows: "In the light of what Paul says about Jesus in general it is safe to assert that his use of our word is to bring out both that Jesus in his earthly career was similar to sinful men and yet not absolutely like them."[51] In other words, through his careful combination of terms, Paul purposed to emphasize two truths concerning Jesus Christ: First, through incarnation Christ became as fully human as other human beings; but, second, He did not become a *sinful* human being. "No other combination of terms could have fulfilled these purposes so perfectly."[52] The fact that Adam was fully human but not sinful before his fall demonstrates that a person does not have to be sinful in order to be fully human.

Impeccability

The third issue related to the sinlessness of Jesus Christ is this: Was Jesus Christ peccable or impeccable throughout His earthly life?

The words *peccable* and *impeccable* are derived from the Latin verb *peccare*, which means "to sin," and the Latin noun *peccator*, which means "sinner."[53] In light of these definitions, the word *peccable*, as applied to Jesus Christ, means "able to sin"; and the word *impeccable*, in relationship to Him, means "not able to sin."

True Christians agree that Jesus Christ never sinned. Christ Himself claimed He never sinned (Jn. 8:46). Christians disagree, however, concerning whether or not He was able to sin. Some believe that, because

Christ was fully human, He was able to sin (was peccable). Others are convinced that, because He was also absolute deity, He was not able to sin (was impeccable). This latter teaching appears to have several problems.

Problem 1: Susceptibility to Sin. The incarnate Jesus Christ was a sinless human being with a sinless human nature, but so was Adam before his fall. The fact that Adam fell away from God indicates he was able to sin. If Adam was susceptible to sinning while being a sinless human being with a sinless human nature, then was not Jesus Christ, "the last Adam" (1 Cor. 15:45), also susceptible to sinning?

The incarnate Jesus Christ had something that Adam did not have—a divine nature. Thus He was fully God as well as fully man. Because holiness is one of the basic attributes of the divine nature, it is impossible for God to sin. Because Christ had a complete divine nature as well as a complete human nature and because deity is far more powerful than humanity, certainly Christ's deity overruled any susceptibility to sin that may have been in the human nature. Christ's deity made it impossible for Him to sin as a person. Thus, as a person, Jesus Christ was not susceptible to sinning.

Problem 2: Still Human or Not. The second problem is this: If the divine nature of Christ overruled His human nature, then were not the attributes of the human nature violated and didn't this action cause Him to cease being human?

Because Adam had a complete human nature but no sin prior to the fall, it is evident that sin is not an essential attribute of the human nature. Human nature can be fully human without sin. Thus, if a divine nature prevents a sinless human nature from sinning, it is not violating any attribute of that human nature. It is simply keeping that human nature what it has always been—a sinless human nature.

The reverse, however, would not be the same. Because holiness is an essential attribute of the divine nature, if the human nature were to overrule the divine nature and cause Christ to sin as a person, the divine nature would be violated and Christ would cease being divine.

Problem 3: Temptation. If Christ was not able to sin, then are not the Scriptures wrong to say that Christ was tempted by Satan (Mk. 1:13) and that He "was in all points tempted like as we are" (Heb. 4:15)? If He was not susceptible to sinning as we are, was He truly tempted in all points as we are?

Temptation is not the same as susceptibility to sin. To tempt means "to allure, appeal strongly to, or invite."[54] Thus temptation is the invitation or solicitation to sin. By contrast, to be susceptible means to be "capable of being affected by" something.[55] Thus susceptibility is the capability of responding to the invitation (temptation) to sin. Jesus Christ was truly tempted (invited to sin) both by Satan and circumstances during His life on earth; but, as a person, He was not capable of responding to the invitation to sin.

Christ could be tempted (invited to sin) in the realm of His humanity, but we must conclude He could not be tempted in the realm of His deity because the Bible states that "God cannot be tempted with evil" (Jas. 1:13). His deity was impeccable (incapable of being invited to sin and incapable of accepting the invitation).

Thus, as a theanthropic person (a God-Man), Jesus Christ was temptable in His humanity but was not capable of sinning. Any influence through the temptability of His humanity was overruled by the impeccability of His deity. In addition, as noted previously, Christ did not have a sin nature prompting Him to respond to the temptations. The apostle John signified this fact when he wrote concerning Christ, "In him is no sin" (1 Jn. 3:5).

In conjunction with the issue of Christ's impeccability, the comments of Matthew and Mark in relation to Satan's tempting of Christ immediately after His baptism are enlightening. Mark wrote, "And immediately the Spirit driveth him into the wilderness. And he was there in the wilderness forty days, tested by Satan" (Mk. 1:12–13a). Matthew's comment reveals the purpose of the Holy Spirit's action: "Then was Jesus led up by the Spirit into the wilderness to be tested by the devil" (Mt. 4:1). The combination of the strong word translated "driveth" and the statement of purpose for the Spirit's action indicates that God wanted this confrontation to take place between His incarnate Son and Satan when Jesus was about to begin His public ministry. God had a purpose for His Son's being subjected to the most intense temptations possible to humanity, administered by the most skilled and powerful tempter possible, while under the most extreme conditions of human deprivation possible (when His humanity would be most temptable).

God's purpose was to demonstrate His Son's impeccability—the fact that as a person He could not sin, even when His humanity was subjected to the most intense temptations from the most skilled, powerful tempter, while it was most vulnerable, over an extended period of time. This demonstration of Jesus Christ's impeccability clearly identified Him as the sinless, spotless Lamb of God, the only person qualified to take away the sin of the world.

PROOF OF CHRIST'S IMPECCABILITY

Scripture gives us a number of proofs for the position that Jesus Christ was incapable of sinning.

His Immutability Requires It

Because Christ is immutable (unchangeable, Heb. 13:8), all the attributes of deity He had *before* His incarnation He continued to have *in* His incarnation. One attribute of deity is holiness, which makes it impossible for God to sin. This divine attribute made it impossible for Christ to sin before His incarnation. Thus His immutability required that it be equally impossible for Him to sin as a person in His incarnation.

His Omnipotence Requires It

Because Christ's divine nature was both holy and omnipotent, it certainly would use its omnipotence to prevent Christ from sinning. Because His human nature was not omnipotent, it could never overrule the omnipotence of His divine nature. Thus Christ *could not* sin because He had an infinitely powerful divine nature that hated sin.

The Sovereignty of God Requires It

Whatever God sovereignly decrees is certain to happen. The Scriptures declare that God "doeth according to his will in the army of heaven, and among the inhabitants of the earth, and none can stay his hand, or say unto him, What doest thou?" (Dan. 4:35). God Himself said, "This is the purpose that is purposed upon the whole earth, and this is the hand that is stretched out upon all the nations. For the LORD of hosts hath purposed, and who shall annul it? And his hand is stretched out, and who shall turn it back?" (Isa. 14:26–27).

In eternity past God sovereignly decreed a plan for history (Eph. 3:11). The fulfillment of that plan centered in the person and redemptive work of the incarnate Jesus Christ (Rev. 13:8). For this reason, Jesus said "he must go unto Jerusalem . . . and be killed, and be raised again the third day" (Mt. 16:21). The word translated "must" refers to what is necessary[56] and relates to God's will, "which fashions history according to its plan."[57] Thus it "expresses a necessity which lies in the very nature of God and which issues in the execution of His plans."[58] Jesus' statement indicated that, for God's plan for history to be fulfilled, it was necessary that He complete the work of redemption through His death and resurrection.

For Jesus Christ to complete that work, He had to be totally sinless. Thus the fulfillment of God's plan for history was dependent on the incarnate Jesus Christ's not sinning. If there had been any possibility Jesus could have sinned, the fulfillment of God's plan would have been uncertain. The fact that God's sovereign decrees are *certain* to be fulfilled required the impossibility of Christ's sinning.

CONCLUSION

Jesus Christ was totally sinless. He never failed to conform perfectly to the holy character and will of God. He did not possess a sin nature; never committed a wrong act; never had a wrong thought, attitude, intent, or impulse; and never failed to do the good deeds that should have been done.

But He loved us so much that He took the penalty for our sin, so we can spend eternity with Him. Have you thanked Him for doing so lately?

CHAPTER FIFTEEN

JESUS CHRIST AND THE FUTURE KINGDOM OF GOD

God created man in his own image" and gave him "dominion . . . over all the earth," including its plant and animal life (Gen. 1:26–29). The fact that God gave mankind this dominion reveals the original form of government He ordained for our planet—a theocracy.

The term *theocracy* means "God-rule" and refers to a form of government in which God's rule is administered by a representative.[1] God created Adam to be His earthly representative, to administer His rule in accord with His will over this earthly province of His universal Kingdom. In order to represent God, Adam had to be in God's image.

Radical Change of Great Consequence

Sometime after God established this earthly theocratic Kingdom, His enemy, Satan, successfully persuaded Adam to join him in his revolt against God (Gen. 3:1–6). As a result, Adam fell away from God, resulting in several tragic consequences. First, because God's earthly representative had defected from Him, the theocracy was lost from planet earth. Second, through Adam's defection, Satan usurped the rule of the world system away from God. Thus God's lost theocratic Kingdom was replaced by a satanocracy, and Satan's rule has continued to dominate the world system ever since the fall of mankind.

Several facts in the Bible make this radical change evident. First, when Satan tempted Jesus, he had the authority to cause all the kingdoms of the world system to pass in visionary form before the Lord and offer the rule of those kingdoms to Him. He told Christ that he had that authority because the rule of the world system had been delivered to him (Lk. 4:5–6). Because Adam was the person to whom God originally gave that rule, he was the one who handed it over to God's enemy when he joined Satan in his revolt against God.

Second, during His first coming, Jesus called Satan "the prince of this world" (Jn. 12:31; 14:30; 16:11). The word translated "prince" means ruler.[2]

Third, the apostle Paul called Satan "the god of this age" (2 Cor. 4:4). As such, Satan blinds the minds of people against ultimate reality and truth through his deceptive false philosophies, which dominate and drive the world system. (See also 2 Corinthians 11:3 and Ephesians 6:11–12.)

Fourth, the apostle John declared that "the whole world lieth in wickedness" (1 Jn. 5:19; cf. Gal. 1:4). The word translated "wickedness" can also be translated "the wicked one." The facts that the definite article *the* is in the Greek text and John clearly referred to the "wicked one" in the immediately preceding verse (1 Jn. 5:18) strongly favor the translation "the wicked one." This would indicate that the world system lies in the sphere of Satan's domain.

Fifth, James asked, "Know ye not that the friendship of the world is enmity with God?" Then he warned, "Whosoever, therefore, will be a friend of the world is the enemy of God" (Jas. 4:4). The verb translated "will" in the warning carries the force of intending or purposing.[3] Thus, by intentionally purposing to be a friend of the world system, a person is made an enemy of God. This is so because God's great enemy, Satan, dominates the present world system. In similar manner, John wrote, "Love not the world, neither the things that are in the world. If any man love the world, the love of the Father is not in him" (1 Jn. 2:15).

Sixth, the Scriptures assert that believers are "strangers and pilgrims on the earth" (Heb. 11:13; cf. 1 Pet. 2:11). Jesus indicated that the world hates His followers because they do not belong to the world system, even though they are in it (Jn. 15:18–19; 17:14–18). Peter warned believers to be vigilant because their adversary, the Devil, walks about like a roaring lion, seeking to devour them (1 Pet. 5:8–9). These statements imply that believers are in enemy territory while living in the present world system.

Another tragic consequence of Adam's joining Satan's revolt against God is the fact that all of nature came under a curse. God told Adam that the ground was cursed because of his defection, now it would produce thorns and thistles, and by the sweat of his brow he would till the ground to grow food (Gen. 3:17–19). Apparently the curse radically reduced the fertility of the soil from its original level.

The animal realm also came under the curse. Before the fall of mankind, all animals were tame and vegetarians; but through the curse many became wild and flesh-eating. For this reason, the apostle Paul wrote, "the creation was made subject to vanity, not willingly," "the whole creation" groans and travails in pain, and eventually "the creation itself also shall be delivered from the bondage of corruption" (Rom. 8:19–22).

Satan's Motivation and History's Purpose

Satan worked to persuade Adam to join him in his revolt against God because he was motivated by the desire to be "like the Most High" (Isa. 14:12–14). Because God was the ultimate sovereign of the universe, Satan wanted to be the ultimate sovereign. But there can be only one ultimate sovereign. Thus Satan's goal was to overthrow God and usurp His position. To accomplish that goal, he began to wage war against God. Because God had His sovereign rule of the earth administered by a human representative, Satan determined to usurp that rule from God by persuading His human representative to defect to him.

This was one of Satan's many attacks in his war against God throughout history. This continuing warfare between Satan and God is the key to discerning the ultimate purpose of world history. Satan's purpose is to overthrow God and usurp His place as the ultimate sovereign of the universe. God's purpose (and, therefore, the ultimate purpose) is to glorify Himself by demonstrating that He alone is the ultimate sovereign.

The Scriptures reveal that, in order to fulfill His purpose for history, God must do three things before the history of this present earth ends. First, He must crush his enemy, Satan, by ridding the earth of him and his world-system rule. Because Satan usurped the rule of this earth's world system away from God, God must rid the earth of Satan and his rule before its history comes to an end; or His enemy would defeat Him within the scope of the present earth's history.

In light of this need to crush Satan, we must note a significant fact. Immediately after Satan succeeded in getting God's representative, Adam, to defect, God informed His enemy that the woman's "seed" would "bruise" his "head" (Gen. 3:15). The word translated "bruise" means "crush."[4] God used language that fit the serpent form Satan took when he tempted mankind to defect from God. If a human being brings his heel down hard on a serpent's head, the serpent's head will be crushed. Through this language, God indicated that in the future, a human offspring of a woman would do God's work of crushing Satan. Later God revealed that the person who would crush the forces of Satan's world system would be His Son, the Messiah ("his anointed," Ps. 2:2, 7–9; cf. Isa. 11:4; Zech. 14:2–3, 12–15).

Second, after God eliminates Satan and his world-system rule, He must restore His own theocratic Kingdom rule to the earth. Because the earth began with God's theocracy as its government, God must restore that rule to the earth before its history comes to an end; or, again, He would be defeated within the scope of the present earth's history. The restoration of God's theocratic Kingdom as the government of earth for its last age of history is absolutely essential to fulfill God's purpose for world history.

Thus, before the history of the present earth comes to an end, God must once again have a man, an Adam, functioning as His representative, administering His rule over this earthly province of His universal Kingdom. In the Old Testament Scriptures, God revealed that He would have such a man. In addition to being God's Son and the Messiah (Ps. 2:2, 7), God's King—who will rule the whole earth in the future (Ps. 2:6, 8; Zech. 14:9)—would also be a man. He would be a child born (Isa. 9:6–7), a biological descendant of David (Isa. 9:7; Jer. 23:5), and "the Son of man" (Dan. 7:13–14). The combination of these facts indicated that, in order to be the future Adam, God's Son would be incarnated in human flesh.

The third thing God must do to fulfill His purpose for history before this present earth comes to an end is remove the curse from nature and thereby restore nature to the way it was before man's fall. Through the Old Testament prophets, God foretold ways in which nature will be transformed in conjunction with the Messiah's future theocratic Kingdom.

For example, God revealed that during the Messiah's righteous reign (Isa. 11:1–5), animal nature will be restored to its original pre-fall condition (Isa. 11:6–9). Once again all animals will be tame and vegetarians. Sheep, goats, and cows will dwell in peace with wolves, leopards, lions, and bears. Children will play at the openings of the dens of snakes, which today are deadly poisonous, without being hurt (Isa. 11:8–9a).

Identification of the Future Adam

New Testament Scriptures record information that identifies Jesus Christ as the future Adam whom God foretold in the Old Testament. First, various witnesses acknowledged that Jesus was the Son of God: God Himself (Mt. 3:17), the angel Gabriel (Lk. 1:26–27, 35), demons (Mt. 8:28–29; Lk. 4:41), and human beings (Mt. 16:16). Second, a holy angel, demons, and human beings recognized He was the Messiah, the Christ (Mt. 16:16; Lk. 2:10–11; 4:41; Jn. 1:40–41). Third, Jesus came into the world as a child born of a woman (Mt. 2:1–11; Lk. 1:26–35; 2:1–17; Gal. 4:4).

Fourth, Jesus' genealogy, the angel Gabriel, and human beings testified that He was a biological descendant of David (Mt. 15:22; 20:30; Lk. 1:32; 3:23–31; Rom. 1:3). Fifth, Jesus claimed to be the Son of man (Mt. 9:6; 16:13; 24:30). Sixth, the apostle Paul called Jesus "the last Adam" (1 Cor. 15:45). The combination of these facts indicated that Jesus Christ was God's Son who became incarnated in human flesh in order to be the future Adam foretold by God (cf. Jn. 1:1, 14; Phil. 2:5–8; Heb. 2:14).

The first Adam lost God's theocratic Kingdom from the earth by joining Satan's revolt. In the future, Jesus Christ, the last Adam, will perform several actions. First, He will crush Satan (Heb. 2:14; 1 Jn. 3:8) by unleashing judgments on Satan's world system (Rev. 6—18), destroying the human leaders and military forces of that system (Rev. 19:11–21), removing all the human members of Satan's kingdom (Mt. 13:36–43, 47–50), and imprisoning Satan in the bottomless pit (Rev. 20:1–3).

Second, He will restore the theocratic Kingdom of God to this earth and, as God's representative, administer God's rule over this earthly province of His universal Kingdom for the last age of earth's history (Rev. 20:4–6). Third, when Christ restores the theocracy, He will regenerate nature, thereby removing its curse, as God foretold through the Old Testament prophets (Acts 3:19–21).

CONCLUSION

Through Jesus Christ the Messiah, God will one day take back rule of His Kingdom on earth, reinstating the theocracy with which it was first governed and removing the curse on nature that came with man's fall. Until that time, we look forward to and pray for His Kingdom to come (Mt. 6:10).

CHAPTER SIXTEEN

JESUS CHRIST
AND THE SEALED SCROLL

As a result of the first Adam's joining Satan's revolt against God, God's theocratic Kingdom was lost from the earth, Satan usurped the rule of the world system away from God, and he has continued to dominate the world system ever since. To fulfill His purpose for history, God must crush Satan by ridding the earth of him and his world-system rule and then restore His theocratic Kingdom rule to this earth before its history ends. In the future, Jesus Christ, as the last Adam, will crush Satan and restore the theocracy.

A critical item related to this future work of Christ is the sealed scroll of Revelation 5.

IDENTIFICATION OF THE SEALED SCROLL

Setting

In Revelation 4 and 5, which records John's introduction to events that "must" take place in the future (4:1), the apostle saw Christ take a scroll from the hand of God the Father. The scroll was sealed with seven seals. Christ took the scroll, so He could break its seals, open it, and read what was written inside (5:1–7). The identification of the sealed scroll is critical to an understanding of future events revealed in Revelation 6–20.

To discern that identification, we must observe several facts emphasized in Revelation 4 and 5.

First, Revelation 4:11 emphasizes that God "created all things" that have been created and He created them for His own benefit or purpose.

Second, God's power or authority to rule all of creation is emphasized in two ways in chapters 4 and 5. First, God's throne is mentioned 17 times. The word for throne indicates dominion or sovereignty.[1]

Also the doxologies in 4:11 and 5:13 use two words to ascribe great power to God. One of those words, *kratos* (5:13), sometimes "is designed to stress the power of God which none can withstand and which is sovereign over all. . . . It denotes the superior power of God to which the final victory will belong."[2]

The other word, *dunamis* (4:11), was used in statements that express "the hope and longing that God will demonstrate His power in a last great conflict, destroying His opponents and saving those who belong to Him. Thus the righteous wait for God to reveal Himself in power and definitively to establish His dominion."[3]

These words portray a divine power that is active in history, a power that shapes and sets a goal for history in accordance with God's own sovereign will and purpose.[4]

Third, Revelation 5:9 and 12 portray Christ as the Redeemer. These verses emphasize His work of redemption through His death and shed blood and that He alone is worthy to take the scroll from God's hand, break its seals, open it, and read it because of His work of redemption.

Fourth, Revelation 5:12–13 points out Christ's worthiness as the Redeemer to exercise God's ruling power. The same power words for God's rule noted earlier are ascribed to Him. In fact, in 5:13 one of those words is used jointly for God and Christ.

Because these four facts are emphasized in the portion of Revelation that introduces the sealed scroll, we can draw a conclusion. The identification of the sealed scroll must relate to the facts that God created all of creation for His own benefit and purpose; He has the power or authority to rule all of creation; and, as the Redeemer, Christ alone is worthy to take the scroll from Gods' hand, break its seals, open and read it, and exercise God's ruling power.

Background

Scripture teaches that because God created the earth and everything in it, He is its owner and sovereign King (Ex. 19:5; 1 Chr. 29:11; Ps. 24:1–2; 47:2–3, 7–9).

When God established His theocracy, He gave His earth to mankind as an inheritance forever (Gen. 1:26–28; Ps. 115:16; Isa. 24:5 ["the everlasting covenant"]). Mankind, however, was not to be regarded as sole owner and authority of the earth. Because God was the ultimate owner, mankind was responsible to serve as His representative, administering His rule over earth for His benefit in accord with His sovereign purpose and in obedience to His commands (Gen. 2:15–17). God was the landlord; mankind was the tenant possessor.

Therefore, mankind did not have the right or authority to forfeit tenant possession or administration of God's earth to anyone else (to a nonkinsman). Tragically, mankind did forfeit tenant possession of their earth inheritance to Satan (a nonkinsman of mankind) by following his lead to rebel against God (Gen. 3). Satan thereby usurped tenant possession of the earth from its original tenant (mankind) and, therefore, from God. He has exercised administrative control of the world system against God ever since.

Mankind's loss is temporary because God has established a program of redemption to prevent this loss from being permanent. This program is based on the work of a kinsman-redeemer (a relative of the same human kind as mankind). That Kinsman-Redeemer is the incarnate Jesus Christ.

As the Kinsman-Redeemer, Christ had to pay a redemption price to redeem mankind and its forfeited inheritance. The price was the shedding of His blood (Eph. 1:7; Col. 1:14; 1 Pet. 1:18–19; Rev. 5:9).

Although Christ paid the redemption price, He will not return the administration of the whole earth to Adam, the man who forfeited mankind's inheritance. As the Kinsman-Redeemer and last Adam, Christ will keep the earth to administer it for God's purposes (Rev. 11:15). Christ "shall be king over all the earth; in that day shall there be one LORD" (Zech. 14:9).

Conclusion

In light of the information Revelation 4 and 5 emphasize and the background of the sealed scroll, we can conclude that the sealed scroll of Revelation 5 is the deed of purchase for mankind's tenant-possession inheritance of the earth, which was forfeited when mankind fell away from God. Just as scroll deeds of purchase were made when Jeremiah paid the redemption price to redeem his cousin's tenant possession of land (Jer. 32:6–12), so a scroll deed of purchase was made when Christ paid the redemption price to redeem mankind's tenant possession of the earth by shedding His blood. Alfred Jenour wrote, "We regard it as a COVENANT DEED, the book in which were registered the terms of man's redemption, and his restoration to the dominion of the earth and all those privileges which he had forfeited by transgression."[5]

Jeremiah's scrolls were legal evidence of his payment of the redemption price and, therefore, of his right of tenant possession of the land. The word translated "deed" *(evidence)* in Jeremiah 32:12 was used for important legal documents that were usually in scroll form.[6] In the same manner, Christ's scroll deed is legal evidence of His payment of the redemption price and, therefore, of His right of tenant possession of the earth.

NEED FOR THE SEALED SCROLL DEED

One of Jeremiah's scroll deeds was sealed to prevent anyone from changing its contents. That gave the scroll the nature of irrefutable evidence. Gottfried Fitzer wrote, "The seal served as a legal protection and guarantee in many ways, esp. in relation to property."[7] Parallel to this purpose, the scroll deed of Revelation 5 is sealed with seven seals, giving that deed the nature of irrefutable legal evidence that Christ is the Kinsman-Redeemer who has the right to take tenant possession of earth.

Jeremiah's scroll deeds were placed in a secure place where they could be preserved for a long period of time because he did not take actual possession of the land immediately after paying the redemption price. Circumstances removed him far from the land for many years. In like manner, Christ's scroll deed was placed in a secure place (God's right hand in heaven, Rev. 5:1, 7) for a long period of time because He did not take actual possession of the earth immediately after paying the redemption price at the cross. He moved to a location far from earth (heaven, Acts 1:9–11) for many years.

As squatters controlled the land of Israel (including the land Jeremiah had purchased) for many years while the Jews and Jeremiah were removed from it, so squatters (Satan and the human members of his kingdom) are controlling the world system during the years Christ is removed from the earth.

TWO RESPONSIBILITIES OF THE KINSMAN-REDEEMER

Land redemption in Israel involved two responsibilities for a kinsman-redeemer. First, he had to pay the redemption price for the forfeited land and thereby obtain the right of tenant possession. Second, he had to take actual possession of the land and exercise administrative rule over it. Sometimes doing so required him to evict squatters who had begun to exercise tenant possession of the land illegally.

In like manner, the redemption of earth involves the same two responsibilities for Christ, mankind's Kinsman-Redeemer. First, He had to pay the redemption price for the earth and thereby obtain the right of tenant possession. Second, now that Christ has obtained that right, He must take actual possession of the earth and exercise authoritative rule over it. This will require Him to evict the squatters—Satan and his forces—who have exercised illegal tenant possession since mankind's fall.

SIGNIFICANCE OF CHRIST'S ACTION WITH THE SEALED SCROLL

If illegal tenants challenged an Israelite kinsman-redeemer's right to take tenant possession of land, the redeemer had to produce legal evidence that he had paid the redemption price and, therefore, had the right to take possession. The sealed scroll deed of purchase was that legal evidence.

Christ will return to the earth to take tenant possession at His Second Coming after the end of the 70th week of Daniel 9. By then, Satan and his forces will have drawn the rulers and armies of the world into the land of Israel to fight against Christ (Ps. 2:1–3; Rev. 16:12–16; 19:11–21). This will be Satan's ultimate challenge to Christ's right to take tenant possession of the earth and to rule it.

This challenge will require Christ to provide irrefutable legal evidence of His right of tenant possession before He evicts the illegal tenants and takes possession. His sealed scroll deed will be that evidence. At the beginning of the seven-year 70th week, Christ will take that deed from God's hand and begin to break its seven seals one by one. He thereby will instigate three series of judgments that will devastate significant areas of Satan's earthly domain (Rev. 6—18) and will demonstrate that He has the power necessary to evict Satan and his forces.

CONCLUSION

As a result of having broken all seven seals during the 70th week, Christ will have the scroll deed open by the time of His Second Coming. At that time He will read the contents of the scroll publicly as the conclusive legal evidence that He is the true Kinsman-Redeemer of mankind's forfeited inheritance and, therefore, has the right to evict Satan and his forces and take tenant possession of earth (Ps. 2:7–9). After presenting this evidence, Christ will fully exercise that right by ridding the earth of Satan and his forces and taking rule of the earth as the last Adam (Rev. 19:19—20:6).

CHAPTER SEVENTEEN

JESUS CHRIST'S CRUSHING OF SATAN

In order to fulfill His purpose for history, God must do three things before the history of planet earth comes to an end. The first of these actions will involve God's crushing of Satan by ridding the earth of him and his entire kingdom. Scripture reveals that God will do so through the combination of the seven-year Tribulation (70th week of Dan. 9:27) and the Second Coming of Christ to earth after the Tribulation. This chapter focuses attention on this combination.

The Tribulation

Jesus Christ will play the key role in crushing Satan. His work of redemption through His death on the cross in His First Coming gives Him the authority to do this future work as mankind's Kinsman-Redeemer (Heb. 2:14; 1 Jn. 3:8).

Seven years before His Second Coming to earth, Christ will take the sealed scroll (the deed of purchase for mankind's forfeited inheritance of tenant possession of the earth) from God's hand in heaven. He will begin to open the scroll by breaking its seven seals one at a time, thereby unleashing three series of divine judgments on planet earth: seven seal judgments (Rev. 6:1—8:1), seven trumpet judgments (Rev. 8:2—11:19), and seven bowl judgments (Rev. 15—16).

These judgments will involve an outpouring of God's wrath on Satan's domain, wreaking havoc on large areas of the earth and great masses of humanity. Just as a modern-day armed force inflicts a heavy, prolonged bombardment on an enemy's domain before invading it, so Christ will inflict this heavy, seven-year bombardment on Satan's earthly domain in preparation for His invasion of it at His Second Coming.

In conjunction with this action, the apostle John recorded a dramatic event that will occur when the seventh trumpet judgment is administered. It will consist of the entire third series of judgments (the seven bowls), significant because it will unleash the last series of judgments that will complete the bombardment and culminate with the Second Coming of Christ, the complete end of Satan's rule, and the establishment of God's future theocratic Kingdom on earth.

Because of the significance of the seventh trumpet, when God's creatures in heaven see it unleashed, they will be so excited in anticipation of the dramatic change it will trigger for the world that they will burst forth with a cry of victory: "The kingdom of this world is become the kingdom of our Lord, and of his Christ, and he shall reign forever and ever" (Rev. 11:15). The verb translated "is become" is a proleptic aorist.[1] This means that, although God's theocratic rule over the world system will not be established until after this last series of judgments has run its course, it will be so certain to happen that God's heavenly creatures can regard it as already accomplished.

THE SECOND COMING

After Christ's Tribulation bombardment of Satan's earthly domain ends, He will invade that domain by coming from heaven to earth with His holy angels in His glorious Second Coming (Mt. 24:29–30; 25:31). Initially He will come to complete the work of crushing Satan by ridding the earth of him and his entire kingdom. Thus He will come in righteousness to "judge and make war" (Rev. 19:11).

As a result of having broken all seven seals during the Tribulation, Christ will have the scroll deed open by the time of His Second Coming. At that time He will read the contents of the scroll publicly as the legal evidence that He is the true Kinsman-Redeemer of mankind's forfeited inheritance and, therefore, has the right to evict Satan and his kingdom and take tenant possession of the earth (Ps. 2:7–9; Rev. 5:4–5). After presenting this evidence, Christ will fully exercise that right. His work of evicting Satan and his kingdom from the earth will involve three phases.

Crushing of Satan's Political and Military System

First, Christ will rid the earth of all the political and military aspects of Satan's world system. When the sixth bowl judgment is poured out on earth, Satan, the Antichrist (Satan's ultimate political world ruler), and the False Prophet will send demons (evil angels) throughout the world to prompt political rulers of all Gentile nations to gather together with their armed forces to one location—the land of Israel (Rev. 16:12–16).

Zechariah 12—14 indicates that these rulers and forces will come against Jerusalem and begin to destroy it. The sixth bowl will be the next-to-the-last judgment of the Tribulation. Therefore, these rulers and armed forces will not begin to gather to Israel until near the end of that seven-year period.

Satan will want the combined might of the rulers and armed forces of the entire Gentile world gathered together in the land of Israel at the city of Jerusalem by the end of the Tribulation for two reasons. First, as a result of Christ's bombardment of his earthly domain throughout the Tribulation and his confinement to earth for the second half of that seven-year period, Satan will recognize that his time is growing short before Christ comes to finish his judgment (Rev. 12:7–12).

Zechariah 14:3–4 reveals that when Christ comes in His Second Coming, He will descend first to the Mount of Olives in the immediate vicinity of Jerusalem. Consequently, Satan will want the combined might of the rulers and armed forces of the Gentile world gathered there to help him try to prevent Christ from returning to earth. He knows that if Christ gets back to earth, his own rule on this planet will be finished. Thus the Antichrist, the False Prophet, political rulers, and armies of the entire Gentile world will be gathered together to make war against Christ and His heavenly army when He comes out of heaven (Rev. 19:11, 19–20; cf. Ps. 2).

Satan's second reason for wanting all the Gentile rulers and military gathered together in Israel by the end of the Tribulation will be to use them as his instruments to try to annihilate Israel totally. Zechariah 12—14 indicates that God will not fully crush Satan, end his evil rule, and establish His theocratic Kingdom rule over the world until the nation of

Israel repents by recognizing and trusting Jesus Christ as its Messiah and Savior. (See Acts 3:12–21.) To Satan's way of thinking, if Israel must repent before God fully crushes him, then he can prevent God from crushing him by totally annihilating Israel before it repents.

Through the gathered political and military powers of the Gentile world, Satan will destroy two-thirds of the Jews in the land of Israel (Zech. 13:8). It will look as if all the Jewish people there will perish. However, before that can happen, Christ will come out of heaven in His glorious Second Coming. When the one-third remnant of Jews left in the land looks on Him and sees the wounds of His crucifixion in His resurrection body, they will repent (change their minds concerning Him). They will recognize and trust Him as their Messiah and Savior (Zech. 12:10–14), and God will cleanse them of their sin (Zech. 13:1). Then Christ will go to war (Zech. 14:3, 12–15). He will cast the Antichrist and False Prophet into the Lake of Fire and destroy the Gentile rulers and military forces (Rev. 19:20–21).

Removal of the Ungodly

Christ declared that, just as the tares are gathered and burned in the fire, so at His Second Coming at the end of the age, His holy angels will gather all the living unsaved and cast them into a place of fiery judgment. Then the living saved will enter God's theocratic Kingdom (Mt. 13:24–30, 36–43).

In the parable of the dragnet (vv. 47–50), Christ taught that, in His Second Coming at the end of the age, His holy angels will separate unsaved people who are alive on earth at that time from the saved. They will cast the unsaved into a place of fiery judgment where they will wail and gnash their teeth (v. 50).

Christ taught this truth again in Matthew 24:37–41. There He indicated that the order of events at His Second Coming will be the same as the order of events in Noah's day. Back then, all the unsaved who were alive were taken from the earth in judgment by the flood; and all the saved (Noah and his family) were left on the earth in the ark to enter the next period of world history. Christ said, "So shall also the coming of the Son of man be" (vv. 37, 39).

Then He indicated that at His Second Coming all the living unsaved will be taken from the earth in judgment, and all the saved will be left on the earth to enter the next period of history—the future theocratic Kingdom Age (vv. 40–41). Luke 17:37 makes it clear that those taken at His Second Coming will be taken into the realm of death, and their dead bodies will be devoured by flesh-eating fowl.

Banishment of Satan and His Angels

The third phase of Christ's eviction of Satan and his kingdom will involve the removal of Satan himself and his evil angels (demons). In conjunction with Christ's Second Coming, Satan will be bound and imprisoned in the bottomless pit for the entire 1,000-year theocratic Kingdom Age (Rev. 20:1–3). The evil angels ("the host of the high ones") will be imprisoned in the pit for the long time during which the Lord reigns in Jerusalem (Isa. 24:21–23).

CONCLUSION

Through His activities in conjunction with the seven-year Tribulation and His Second Coming, Christ will complete one of His responsibilities as the Kinsman-Redeemer of mankind's lost inheritance. He will crush Satan, the usurper of that inheritance, by ridding the earth of him and his entire kingdom. He will thereby accomplish the first future thing that God must do to fulfill His purpose for history.

CHAPTER EIGHTEEN

JESUS CHRIST'S RESTORATION OF GOD'S THEOCRATIC KINGDOM

God must accomplish three things to fulfill His purpose for history. The first is crushing Satan by ridding the earth of him and his entire kingdom. The second is restoring His theocratic Kingdom-rule to this present earth.

Purpose of the Future Theocratic Kingdom

Earth began with God's theocracy as its government, but the theocracy was lost through the Satan-prompted fall of mankind. If God does not restore His theocratic Kingdom rule to earth before its history comes to an end, then Satan will have defeated God within the scope of this present earth's history. The restoration of God's theocratic Kingdom as the government of earth for its last age of history is absolutely essential if God is to fulfill His purpose for world history.

Time of the Future Theocratic Kingdom

The Scriptures reveal two things concerning the time of the future theocratic Kingdom. First, the theocratic Kingdom will be established after the Tribulation and Second Coming of Christ. Christ Himself taught that He will sit on His throne to rule the earth and introduce the righteous to the Kingdom after the Tribulation and His Second Coming (Mt. 24:21, 29–30; 25:31–34). The book of Revelation supports Christ's teaching by presenting the following order for the future: the events of the Tribulation (Rev. 6—18), followed by the Second Coming of Christ (Rev. 19:11–21), and then the theocratic Kingdom (Rev. 20:4–6).

Second, the future theocratic Kingdom will be present during the last age of this present earth's history. After that age ends, Satan will lead one final revolt against God's rule; and God will quickly crush that revolt (Rev. 20:7–10). Then the present earth will pass away when a great white throne appears (Rev. 20:11; 21:1).

Length of the Future Theocratic Kingdom

Revelation 20:4–7 indicates that Christ and His saints will reign over this present earth for "a thousand years." Thus the future theocratic Kingdom will last for 1,000 years on this present earth. For this reason, Bible scholars have called the final age of earth's history "the Millennium" (from the Latin words *mille*, which means "a thousand," and *annum*, which means "year").

Although the future theocratic Kingdom will last for 1,000 years on this present earth, it will continue forever on the future eternal earth (Lk. 1:32–33; Rev. 11:15; 21:1—22:5).

CITIZENS OF THE FUTURE THEOCRATIC KINGDOM

The Bible reveals several significant facts concerning the citizens of the future theocratic Kingdom. First, no unsaved people (human members of Satan's kingdom) will be allowed to enter the Kingdom at its inception. All the unsaved who are alive at Christ's Second Coming will be taken from earth in judgment. Jesus clearly taught this fact in His parables of the tares (Mt. 13:24–30, 36–43) and the dragnet (Mt. 13:47–50) and His Olivet Discourse (Mt. 24:37–41; 25:31–46).

Second, all the saved people of all previous ages of history will enter the theocratic Kingdom with Christ. They will consist of four groups.

Church Saints

Those saved from the Day of Pentecost in Acts 2 until the Rapture of the church will constitute the first group. Because they will have been

152

raptured to heaven before the Tribulation, they will return with Christ to the earth at His Second Coming following the Tribulation. Thus they will be on earth with Him for the theocratic Kingdom.

Two teachings indicate this fact. First, after the apostle Paul referred to the church saints being raptured from the earth to meet Christ in the air, he said, "And so shall we ever be with the Lord" (1 Th. 4:17). Once raptured, the church saints will go wherever Christ goes. Second, Paul also taught that church saints shall reign with Christ (2 Tim. 2:12). As a result of the transformation of their bodies at the Rapture (1 Cor. 15:51–53; 1 Th. 4:16), they will have glorified, immortal bodies in the theocratic Kingdom.

Old Testament Saints

Those who became saved and died before the church began will constitute the second group of saints in the theocratic Kingdom. They will be resurrected in conjunction with Christ's Second Coming after the Tribulation. Daniel 12:1–2 refers to people being resurrected to everlasting life after the unparalleled time of trouble (the Great Tribulation). A statement made to Daniel in that context seems to indicate that he, as an Old Testament saint, would be resurrected at that time (12:13).

Resurrected Tribulation Saints

These will constitute the third group in the theocratic Kingdom. The apostle John indicated that people who will become saved and be martyred during the Tribulation will be resurrected in conjunction with the Second Coming of Christ after the Tribulation (Rev. 20:4–6).

Surviving Tribulation Saints

This fourth group of saints entering the theocratic Kingdom will be comprised of people who will become saved during the Tribulation and will survive that period alive. Because they will have escaped death, they will enter the Kingdom with mortal bodies and, therefore, will still have their sin natures. They also will be able to marry and give birth to children. These surviving saints are "the sheep" of Matthew 25:31–34 and those that are "left" in the field and at the mill at Christ's Second Coming (Mt. 24:39–41). They will differ markedly from the saints of the first three groups, all of whom will enter the Kingdom with glorified, immortal bodies and, therefore, will be sinlessly perfect and will not marry or give birth to children.

A third significant fact about the citizens of the future theocratic Kingdom is that some will be unsaved. Unsaved children will be born into the Kingdom after its beginning (Jer. 30:19–20; Ezek. 47:22). Thus, although only saved people will be on earth at the beginning of the Kingdom, after a while unsaved people will arrive through childbirth. The fact that a huge multitude will flock to Satan when he is released from the bottomless pit after the Millennium (Rev. 20:7–9) indicates that many of those born during the Millennium will not believe on the Lord.

NATURE OF THE FUTURE THEOCRATIC KINGDOM

Two things should be noted concerning the nature of the future theocratic Kingdom. First, it will be an earthly kingdom involving the administration of God's rule over everything on this present earth. Second, it will be a political kingdom involving governmental structure and function.

Earthly Kingdom

Just as the original theocratic Kingdom involved the administration of God's rule by His original representative, the first Adam, over this present earthly province of God's universal Kingdom, so the future theocratic Kingdom will involve the administration of God's rule by His future representative, the last Adam (Jesus Christ), over this same earthly province.

The following facts give evidence to this truth: After Christ's feet touch down on the Mount of Olives at His Second Coming, He will be King "over all the earth" (Zech. 14:4, 9). His "dominion shall be from sea even to sea, and from the river even to the ends of the earth" (Zech. 9:10). God's future Kingdom will fill "the whole earth" (Dan. 2:35, 44–45).

When Christ will reign as King, He will execute judgment and justice "in the earth," and the people of Israel will "dwell in their own land" (Jer. 23:5–8). When Christ, as the Son of man, will come with the clouds of heaven in His Second Coming, the Kingdom rule that God will give Him and the saints will be the Kingdom "under the whole heaven" (Dan. 7:13–14, 27). The Kingdom that God and Christ will take over in the future will be the Kingdom "of this world" (Rev. 11:15).

After the Millennium, when Satan will lead a final revolt against Christ's future rule, he will deceive the nations located "in the four quarters of the earth" (Rev. 20:7–8). The rebels will go up "on the breadth of the earth" and judgment will come "down from God out of heaven" (v. 9). After this judgment, the present earth will be replaced by a new, eternal earth (Rev. 20:11; 21:1).

Political Kingdom

Evidences for the political nature of the Kingdom are as follows: When Christ will rule, He will sit on David's throne, ruling David's kingdom (Isa. 9:7; Lk. 1:32–33). Since David's kingdom was political in nature, Christ's Kingdom will be also. Isaiah 9:6–7 states that, when Christ will sit on David's throne ruling his kingdom, "the government shall be upon his shoulder," and "of the increase of his government and peace there shall be no end." The term *government* implies literal political rule. There will be individual nations with subkings under the rule of Christ (Ps. 72:10–11, 17). He will be the "KING OF KINGS, AND LORD OF LORDS" (Rev. 19:16).

Christ will exercise control over international relations, causing nations to live together in peace (Isa. 2:4; Mic. 4:3). His capital city, Jerusalem, will be the political center of the world. Out of it will issue forth the law by which the nations will be governed (Isa. 2:1–3; Mic. 4:1–2). As Supreme Judge over the affairs of His subjects, He will protect the poor, needy, and meek and will punish oppressors and execute the wicked (Ps. 72:1–4, 12–14; Isa. 11:1–5). These are the functions of political government (Rom. 13:1–7).

Christ's rule will be characterized by absolute righteousness, justice, and peace (Isa. 9:7). It appears that all His officeholders will be glorified, immortal saints who have no sin nature (2 Tim. 2:12; Rev. 20:4–6). This means that every politician in His government will be sinlessly perfect and, therefore, there will be no government corruption.

CONCLUSION

By restoring God's theocratic Kingdom-rule to this present earth in conjunction with His Second Coming, Christ will accomplish the second future thing that God must do to fulfill His purpose for history.

CHAPTER NINETEEN

JESUS CHRIST'S REMOVAL OF THE CURSE

In order for God to fulfill His purpose for history, He must crush Satan by ridding the earth of him and his entire kingdom and restore His theocratic Kingdom-rule to this present earth. The third thing God must do is remove the curse from nature that came as a tragic consequence of Adam joining Satan's revolt against God. God must restore nature to the way it was before the fall of mankind.

PROPHECIES OF THE RESTORATION

Jesus Christ's Prophecy

Matthew 19:28 records a prophecy Christ delivered to His apostles: "Verily I say unto you that ye who have followed me, in the regeneration, when the Son of man shall sit on the throne of his glory, ye also shall sit upon twelve thrones, judging the twelve tribes of Israel."

The word translated "regeneration" comes from two Greek words— *palin* and *genesis*.[1] The word *palin* means "back" and "again, once more, anew." It refers to the recurrence of "a state of being . . . in the same (or nearly the same) way as at first."[2] Thus Christ foretold a future time when nature will return to its original condition recorded in Genesis, before it was subjected to the curse of mankind's sin.

In Matthew 19:28 Christ indicated that this restoration of nature to its prefall condition will take place when He, as the Son of man, "shall sit on the throne of his glory." A comparison of Matthew 25:31 with 24:29–31 indicates that He will not sit on "the throne of his glory" until His Second Coming after the Tribulation. Thus nature will not be restored to its prefall condition until Christ restores God's theocratic Kingdom-rule to this present earth in conjunction with His Second Coming and then, as God's representative King, administers God's rule over all the earth (Zech. 14:4, 9; Mt. 25:31, 34).

Other Scriptures confirm that this restoration of nature will not take place until the future, theocratic Kingdom when Christ will rule as King. In Matthew 19:28, Christ taught that nature will be regenerated when the apostles "shall sit upon twelve thrones, judging the twelve tribes of Israel." In Luke 22:28–30 the Lord indicated that His apostles will "sit on thrones judging the twelve tribes of Israel" in His Kingdom.

Thus in Matthew 19:28, Christ was prophesying "the renewing of the world in the time of the Messiah . . . *in the new* [Messianic] age."[3]

Apostle Peter's Prophecy

Acts 3:19–21 records prophetic statements the apostle Peter delivered to a crowd of Jewish people in the vicinity of the Temple in Jerusalem sometime after the Day of Pentecost (Acts 3:1–11; cf. Acts 2:1). Peter indicated that, when Israel will get spiritually right with God and His Messiah, their sins will be "blotted out, when the times of refreshing shall come from the presence of the Lord" (Acts 3:19).

The word translated "when" in the expression *when the times of refreshing shall come* indicates purpose.[4] Thus the future times of refreshing cannot come until the people of Israel change their minds concerning Jesus Christ and turn to accept Him as their Messiah and Savior. The expression *the times of refreshing* refers to "the Messianic Age."[5]

The apostle also made it clear that the times of refreshing cannot come until Jesus Christ returns from heaven to be physically present on the earth again (vv. 19–20). Peter emphasized this teaching further by saying of Christ, "Whom the heaven must receive until the times of restitution of all things" (v. 21). Heaven had already received Christ into itself on the day of His ascension, some time before Peter made these Acts 3 statements (Acts 1:9). The word *until* in the expression *until the times of restitution of all things* indicated that Christ would not remain in heaven forever. (See also Acts 1:10–11.) Thus Peter pointed out that the future times of restitution of all things cannot come until Christ returns from heaven to earth in His Second Coming after the Tribulation.

The expressions *the times of refreshing* and *the times of restitution of all things* refer to the same time and "mutually explain one another."[6] Both refer to the future Messianic Age when the Messiah will administer God's rule over the entire earth in the restored, theocratic Kingdom.

In the expression *the times of restitution of all things*, the word translated "restitution" had the following basic meaning in ancient secular usage: "restitution to an earlier state," or "restoration."[7] Concerning its meaning in Peter's Acts 3:21 declaration, Albrecht Oepke wrote, it "cannot denote the conversion of persons but only the reconstitution or establishment of things. . . . These are restored, i.e., brought back to the integrity of creation."[8] In other words, Peter referred to the future restoration of the original order of things that God established on earth at creation.

F. F. Bruce wrote that "the restitution" to which Peter referred in Acts 3:21 "appears to be identical with the *palingenesia* ('regeneration') of Matthew 19:28 . . . the final inauguration of the new age is accompanied by a renovation of all nature (cf. Rom. 8:18–23)."[9] This statement implies that Peter's Acts 3 prophecy and Christ's Matthew 19:28 prophecy refer to the same future restoration of nature to its original, prefall state.

Consequently, in Acts 3:19–21 Peter referred to the future Messianic Age that will begin when Jesus Christ, in conjunction with His Second Coming to earth after the Tribulation, will (1) restore God's theocratic kingdom-rule to the earth and (2) restore nature to its original condition by removing the curse under which it has labored since the fall of mankind.

Apostle Paul's Prophecy

In Romans 8 the apostle Paul declared that in the past, the natural, created realm in which mankind lives was subjected to a cursed existence characterized by "vanity" (no meaningful purpose)[10]: "For the creation was made subject to vanity, not willingly but by reason of him who hath subjected the same in hope" (Rom. 8:20).

This did not happen because of something nature did. Rather, God subjected it to the curse because of the fall of Adam, the human representative whom God had appointed to administer His rule over the earth (v. 20). Paul, therefore, implied that originally nature was not under this curse.

In this cursed existence, nature is enslaved to "corruption" ("decay," v. 21).[11] All parts of mankind's natural realm continue to groan together and suffer the agony of travail (literally, "birth pangs") together (v. 22). Because a woman's birth pangs do not last forever, the metaphor implies that eventually nature will be delivered from this curse.

When God subjected nature to this cursed existence, He did so in hope (v. 20) based on the fact that nature itself will someday be set free from the curse with its slavery to decay (v. 21). Because of this factually based hope, nature eagerly awaits[12] with "earnest expectation" (v. 19). The word translated "earnest expectation" describes "a person leaning forward out of intense interest and desire."[13] It denotes "diversion from other things and concentration on a single object."[14]

The single object on which nature focuses is "the manifestation of the sons of God," because at the time of that manifestation, nature will be freed from its cursed existence (v. 19). Sanday and Headlam note that the word translated "manifestation" is the same word that "is applied to the Second Coming of the Messiah and to that of the redeemed who accompany Him."[15] They also assert that the Messiah will deliver nature "from its ills" in conjunction with His Second Coming.[16] Through the combination of these two items, they indicate that both the manifestation of the sons of God and the deliverance of nature from its cursed existence will take place in conjunction with Christ's Second Coming.

John Murray asserts that the apostle Paul, in Romans 8, prophesied of the same future transformation of nature as the "regeneration" in Jesus Christ's Matthew 19:28 prophecy and the "restitution of all things" in the apostle Peter's Acts 3:21 prophecy.[17]

Old Testament Prophets' Prophecies

In Acts 3 the apostle Peter indicated that, through the Old Testament prophets, God gave revelation concerning the future Messianic-Age restoration of nature to its original prefall condition (v. 21).

The Old Testament prophets foretold miraculous changes that will come to the world when the Messiah will establish and rule over the future theocratic Kingdom of God.

COMPARISON OF CHRIST'S MIRACLES WITH OLD TESTAMENT PROPHECIES

A comparison of Jesus Christ's miracles with Old Testament prophecies concerning the miraculous changes of the future theocratic Kingdom reveals that, through His miracles, Jesus demonstrated to the people of Israel that He was the Messiah—the One who had the powers necessary to fulfill those Old Testament prophecies.

First, the prophets foretold that the future theocratic Kingdom will exhibit beneficial changes in the earth's climate and natural elements (Isa. 30:23–26; Ezek. 47:1–12; Joel 2:21–26; 3:18; Zech. 14:8). The effectiveness of the moon and sun will be increased, and abundant rains will fall when needed. Special streams of water will flow from Jerusalem to cleanse polluted bodies of water and make waste places fruitful. Jesus demon-strated His power to control the earth's climate and natural elements by walking on the water of the Sea of Galilee and calming two storms (Mt. 14:22–33; Mk. 4:35–41).

Second, according to the prophets, the theocratic Kingdom will be characterized by unprecedented growth and fruitage of trees (Isa. 41:19–20; Ezek. 36:8, 30; 47:6–7, 12; Joel 2:21–22). Jesus displayed His power to control the growth and fruitage of trees by cursing a fig tree and causing it to wither immediately (Mt. 21:18–20).

Third, the prophets declared that there will be great productivity of animals, including a huge multitude of fish, during the theocratic Kingdom (Ezek. 36:11; 47:8–10). Twice Jesus miraculously produced a huge draught of fish for His disciples after they had fished all night without catching anything (Lk. 5:1–11; Jn. 21:1–12). Here was evidence that He could produce the great productivity of animals, including the huge multitude of fish, prophesied for the future Messianic Kingdom.

Fourth, the prophets proclaimed that the future theocratic Kingdom will be blessed with a superabundant supply of food (Ps. 72:16; Isa. 30:23–24; Ezek. 34:25–30; Joel 2:21–26; Zech. 8:11–12). Famine will be unknown. Jesus exhibited His power to produce this superabundance by expanding five loaves of bread and two fish into more than enough food to feed 5,000 men. After all these people were filled, there were 12 baskets of food left (Jn. 6:5–14). On another occasion Christ increased seven loaves of bread and several small fish into enough to feed about

4,000 people. After all of them were filled, seven baskets of food were left (Mk. 8:1–9).

Fifth, according to the prophets, wine will be abundant in the future theocratic Kingdom (Joel 2:21–26; Amos 9:13). Jesus manifested His ability to cause this abundance of wine in the future Kingdom when He turned water into wine at a marriage celebration in Cana of Galilee (Jn. 2:1–11).

Sixth, the prophets predicted dramatic changes in the nature of animals in the future theocratic Kingdom (Isa. 11:6–9; 65:25; Hos. 2:18). All animals will be completely tame and vegetarians. Sheep, goats, calves, and cows will dwell together with wolves, leopards, lions, and bears and not be harmed. Instead of being carnivorous, the lion will eat the same vegetation as the ox. Little children will be able to lead all these animals as pets. Poisonous snakes that today are deadly will no longer be harmful.

Jesus demonstrated His ability to change or exercise authority over the nature of animals. On His triumphal entry into Jerusalem, He rode a colt that had never been sat on by a human being. He had no trouble doing so, in spite of the fact that such an animal would normally have attempted to throw off a rider. Jesus changed the nature of that colt (Mk. 11:1–11). On another occasion, He caused a fish to have a specific coin in its mouth and to swim to a specific place, at a specific time, to be caught by Peter (Mt. 17:24–27).

Seventh, the prophets declared that the future theocratic Kingdom will be characterized by the healing of physical diseases and deformities (Is. 29:18; 33:24; 35:5–6). The lame will be made to walk, the blind made to see, the deaf made to hear, and the dumb made to speak. No longer will anyone say, "I am sick."

Jesus gave overwhelming evidence of His power to produce that aspect of the future Kingdom. He healed lame (Mt. 8:5–13; Mk. 2:1–12; Jn. 5:1–9), blind (Mt. 9:27–31; 12:22; 20:29–34; Mk. 8:22–26; Jn. 9:1–7), deaf (Mk. 7:31–37; 9:14–29), and dumb people (Mt. 9:32–34; 12:22; Mk. 7:31–37; 9:14–29). He also healed those at the point of death (Jn. 4:46–54); those possessed by demons (Mt. 9:32–34; 15:21–28; Mk. 1:21–28, 34; 5:1–20; 9:14–29); lepers (Mk. 1:40–45; Lk. 17:11–19); and those with fever (Mk. 1:29–31), withered hands (Mk. 3:1–5), issues of blood (Mt. 9:20–22), infirmity (Lk. 13:10–13), and dropsy (Lk. 14:1–4). He also replaced a severed ear (Lk. 22:50–51). Plus He performed many other miracles of healing that were not specifically recorded (Mt. 4:23–24; 8:16; 9:35; 15:29–31; Mk. 1:34; 6:56; Lk. 4:40; 5:15; 6:17–19; 7:21).

Eighth, the prophets foretold that the future theocratic Kingdom will be marked by great longevity of life (Isa. 65:20–22). The 100-year-old person will be classified as a child; infancy will be measured by years, not days. Old men will live a full life, and the days of God's people will be as the days of a tree. Jesus raised Lazarus, Jairus' daughter, and the widow's son from the dead, thereby lengthening their lives beyond their normal span (Jn. 11:1–45; Mt. 9:18–26; Lk. 7:11–17). This was evidence that He has the power to produce the longevity of life characteristic of the future theocratic Kingdom.

Significance of the Comparison

When the Messiah will establish and rule over the future theocratic Kingdom, miraculous changes will come to the world. By comparing Jesus' miracles with Old Testament prophecies concerning the nature of the future theocratic Kingdom, it is easy to see the relationship between Christ's miracles and those prophecies.

The writer of Hebrews recognized and referred to that relationship. He stated that Jews who were eyewitnesses of Christ's miracles thereby "tasted . . . the powers of the age to come" (Heb. 6:5). Two things should be noted regarding this statement. First, Jesus used the word translated "powers" in reference to His miracles (Mt. 11:20–23). Other people used the same word for His miracles (Mt. 13:54, 58; 14:2; Lk. 19:37; Acts 2:22). Some used it specifically for His miracles of healing illnesses (Mk. 5:30; 6:5; Lk. 5:17; 6:19) and casting out demons (Lk. 4:36). Second, since the book of Hebrews was written during this present, pre-Messianic Age, the writer's expression *the age to come* (Heb. 6:5) refers to the future Messianic Age, when Christ, the Messiah, will establish and rule over the future theocratic Kingdom.

The combination of these two things prompts three conclusions. First, the writer of Hebrews indicated that Christ's miracles were a foretaste of the powers He will exercise when He will transform nature, in fulfillment of Old Testament prophecies, in conjunction with His establishment of the future theocratic Kingdom. Second, those powers are to be associated uniquely with that future Messianic Age, not the present pre-Messianic Age. The fact that nature has not yet experienced that transformation, but still labors under the curse that came with mankind's fall from God, substantiates this conclusion. Third, this foretaste of Christ's powers in the past guarantees that the future theocratic Kingdom, with its transformation of nature, will take place in conjunction with His Second Coming in the future.

Primary Purpose of Christ's Miracles

Christ's miracles demonstrated conclusively that He is the Messiah who will fulfill Old Testament prophecies concerning the future theocratic Kingdom and its transformation of nature. This conclusion is based on several lines of testimony.

Jesus' Testimony. When asked to state plainly if He were the Messiah, Jesus said, "I told you, and ye believed not; the works that I do in my Father's name, they bear witness of me" (Jn. 10:24–25). Later He indicated that witnesses of His miracles had a solemn responsibility to believe His claims (Jn. 15:24).

Apostle John's Testimony. John declared that he recorded some of Jesus' miracles in order that his readers might believe that Jesus is the Messiah, the Son of God (Jn. 20:30–31; see also John 1:41). John also expressed amazement that some eyewitnesses of Jesus' miracles did not, as a result, believe His claim to be the Messiah (Jn. 12:37–38).

Testimony of Jesus' Response to John the Baptist's Question. John's imprisonment caused him to question if Jesus were the Messiah. He sent a message to Jesus, asking if He were the Messiah who was to come. In response, Jesus performed miracles before John's messengers, then sent them to tell John what they had witnessed. The miracles were to assure John that Jesus was, indeed, the Messiah (Lk. 7:19–23).

Apostle Peter's Testimony. Peter declared Jesus to be the Messiah (Acts 2:36) and indicated that God certified Him to be the Messiah "by miracles and wonders and signs, which God did by him" in Israel (v. 22).

CONCLUSION

By restoring nature to its original prefall condition when He restores God's theocratic Kingdom-rule to this present earth, Christ will accomplish the third future thing that God must do to fulfill His purpose for history.

JESUS CHRIST AND THE KINGDOM-OF-GOD CONCEPT

W hen Jesus Christ was on earth during His First Coming, He said, "The kingdom of God is at hand" (Mk. 1:15); and He taught His disciples to pray "thy kingdom come" (Mt. 6:10). In what sense was He referring to the Kingdom of God in these expressions? To answer this question, we must examine the Kingdom-of-God concept in the Bible.

Basis of the Concept

The sovereignty of God is the basis of the concept of the Kingdom of God in the Bible. King David's expression in 1 Chronicles 29:11–12 indicates this truth:

Thine, O LORD, is the greatness, and the power, and the glory, and the victory, and the majesty; for all that is in the heaven and in the earth is thine. Thine is the kingdom, O LORD, and thou art exalted as head above all. Both riches and honor come of thee, and thou reignest over all; and in thine hand is power and might; and in thine hand it is to make great, and to give strength unto all.

Here David declared three facts about God: First, God has sovereign power, or authority, to rule. Second, He has a realm ("all that is in the heaven and in the earth") over which to exercise His sovereign rule. Third,

He actually exercises His sovereign rule over that realm. All three are essentials to have a kingdom. Since God, in His sovereignty, possesses or does all these things, David declared that God has a kingdom.

DISTINCTIONS IN THE CONCEPT

The Bible presents three distinctions in the Kingdom-of-God concept: time, scope, and administration. At first they appear to be contradictions, although they are not.

Time

Some Scriptures present the Kingdom of God as an entity that *has existed continually since God created the universe:* "The LORD hath prepared his throne in the heavens, and his kingdom ruleth over all" (Ps. 103:19); "The LORD reigneth. . . . Thy throne is established of old; thou art from everlasting" (Ps. 93:1–2); "Thou, O LORD, remainest forever, thy throne from generation to generation" (Lam. 5:19). The apostle Paul declared that the God who created all things "is Lord of heaven and earth" (Acts 17:24).

By contrast, however, other Scriptures indicate that the Kingdom of God is *to come in the future;* it is not here yet. Some 600 years before Christ, the prophet Daniel foretold, "And in the days of these kings shall the God of heaven set up a kingdom" (Dan. 2:44). Christ, in fact, taught His disciples to pray that the Kingdom of God would come (Mt. 6:10).

Scope

Some Scriptures present the Kingdom of God as being *universal in scope* with the entire universe as its realm. As noted earlier, David indicated that it includes "all that is in the heaven and in the earth." David also declared that God's "kingdom ruleth over all" (Ps. 103:19; cf. 135:6). The apostle Paul stated that God is "Lord of heaven and earth" (Acts 17:24).

Nevertheless, other Scriptures present the Kingdom of God as being *earthly in scope* with the earth alone as its realm. As recorded in Daniel 2:35, 44–45, the stone—which represented the future Kingdom that God will establish—filled the whole earth. In Daniel 7 the future Kingdom (which God will give to the Son of man, who comes with the clouds of heaven, and to the saints) is described as being "under the whole heaven" (Dan. 7:27). According to Zechariah 14:4 and 9, when the Messiah will come to earth at His Second Coming, "the LORD shall be king over all the earth." The apostle John foresaw creatures of God, during the future Tribulation period, talking about the kingdom (singular in the Greek text) of the world becoming the Kingdom of God and His Christ (Rev. 11:15).

Administration

Some Scriptures present the Kingdom of God as being God's rule administered *directly by Him over any or all parts of the universe*. No human agent administers God's rule on His behalf. For example, it was God, not a human agent, who inflicted King Nebuchadnezzar with insanity (Dan. 4) to demonstrate "that the Most High ruleth in the kingdom of men" (v. 17). Nebuchadnezzar acknowledged that his insanity was an expression of God's Kingdom-rule. And he described the directness of that rule as follows: "He doeth according to his will in the army of heaven, and among the inhabitants of the earth, and none can stay his hand, or say unto him, What doest thou?" (v. 35).

Without the aid of human agents, God killed 185,000 Assyrian soldiers in one night (2 Ki. 19). Concerning this direct administration of His Kingdom-rule, God declared, "Surely . . . as I have purposed, so shall it stand: That I will break the Assyrian in my land. . . . For the Lord of hosts hath purposed, and who shall annul it? And his hand is stretched out, and who shall turn it back?" (Isa. 14:24–25, 27).

But by contrast, other Scriptures present the Kingdom of God as being God's rule administered *indirectly, through a human agent, only over the earth*. Psalm 2:6–9 portrays God establishing the Messiah as King to rule the nations and all parts of the earth. The fact that the Messiah will be God's agent, who will administer God's rule over this earthly province of God's universal Kingdom, is indicated by two facts. First, God calls the Messiah "my king" (v. 6). Second, any rebellion against the Messiah will also be rebellion against God (vv. 2–3) and will bring God's wrath (vv. 4–5).

Daniel 7:13–14 depicts God giving the Son of man a Kingdom over which to rule. This Kingdom will consist of "all people, nations, and languages" (v. 14) and will be "under the whole heaven" (v. 27), meaning limited to this earth. A parallel passage (Dan. 2:44) indicates that this Kingdom is God's Kingdom, for it declares that it is set up by the God of heaven. A comparison of Daniel 2:35 with verses 44 and 45 shows that this Kingdom of God will fill the whole earth. Thus Daniel

2 and 7 describe an earthly Kingdom of God in which God's rule will be administered indirectly by a human agent, the Son of man, who will come with the clouds of heaven.

Similar concepts are presented in Revelation 11:15, which talks about the kingdom of the world becoming the Kingdom of God and of His Christ and then indicates that one of these persons ("he"—singular) will reign. Revelation 19 and 20 clearly signify that Christ is that one person who will come to earth to reign over this Kingdom of God. Here again is the picture of an earthly Kingdom of God in which God's rule is administered indirectly by a human agent, Christ.

Summary

There are, then, three significant distinctions in the biblical concept of the Kingdom of God: *time* (the Kingdom of God has existed continually since God created the universe, but it also has not yet started); *scope* (the Kingdom of God is universal, yet it is only earthly); and *administration* (the Kingdom of God is the rule of God administered directly by Him over any or all parts of the universe, but it also is the rule of God administered indirectly through a human agent over the earth alone).

EXPLANATION OF THESE DISTINCTIONS

In spite of how it may appear, these distinctions are not contradictions. Instead, they indicate that the Kingdom of God has at least two aspects, or expressions.

Universal Kingdom of God

The universal Kingdom of God is the first aspect, or expression. It is God's rule over the entire universe, including the earth, and everything in it. This rule has existed continually since God created the universe.

Dispensations are the different ways in which God administers His universal Kingdom-rule over the earth during its history. It could be said that each dispensation is a particular expression, or phase, of God's universal Kingdom-rule over the earthly province of His universal Kingdom. Sometimes God administers this rule directly (not through a human agent) and sometimes indirectly, through a human agent.

Theocratic Kingdom of God

The theocratic Kingdom of God constitutes the second aspect, or expression, of the Kingdom. A theocracy is the form of government in which a human agent or representative administers God's rule. In light of the nature of a theocracy and the biblical teaching concerning this aspect of the Kingdom of God, we can draw several conclusions concerning the theocratic Kingdom of God.

First, it is a more narrow, or limited, aspect of the Kingdom of God than is the universal Kingdom because the theocratic Kingdom is but one aspect of the universal Kingdom.

Second, the theocratic Kingdom is restricted to God's rule over the earth. It does not involve His rule over the entire universe. By contrast, the universal Kingdom of God concerns God's rule over the entire universe, including the earth.

Third, the theocratic Kingdom of God is restricted to the indirect administration of God's rule through a human agent or representative (an Adam). It does not involve God's direct administration of His rule. By contrast, the universal Kingdom of God involves both the indirect and direct administration of God's rule.

Fourth, the theocratic Kingdom is restricted to those times when God has a human agent (an Adam) administering His rule over the entire earth. There are only two such time periods for this present earth: the time between man's creation and fall and the time of the future Millennium. Thus the theocratic Kingdom constitutes the first and last phases of God's universal Kingdom-rule over this present earth.

CONCLUSION

When God's first human agent, Adam, fell, the first phase of the theocratic Kingdom was lost; Satan usurped the rule of the world system away from God and has dominated that system ever since. It is important to note that God's ownership of the earth and His universal Kingdom-rule over the earth did not end at that time. Only the theocratic-Kingdom phase of His universal Kingdom-rule of the earth ended at the fall of man. Other phases of His universal Kingdom-rule have been present on the earth since that time. Thus, centuries after Adam's rebellion, David could write, "The earth is the LORD's, and the fullness thereof" (Ps. 24:1).

CHAPTER TWENTY-ONE

JESUS CHRIST AND THE GOSPEL OF THE KINGDOM

The Kingdom of God has at least two aspects: the universal and theocratic. Given these distinctions, to which of these aspects of the Kingdom was Jesus Christ referring when He said, "the kingdom of God is at hand" (Mk. 1:15) and when He taught His disciples to pray, "Thy kingdom come" (Mt. 6:10)?

Christ's Reference to the Kingdom

Jesus' statement, "the kingdom of God is at hand," indicated that there was some sense in which the Kingdom was not yet present. The fact that He taught His disciples to pray for God's Kingdom to come indicated the same thing. That prayer was a petition, asking that God's Kingdom come, in some sense, in the future.

Since the universal Kingdom has existed continually since God created the universe, that aspect was already present when Christ indicated that there was still some way in which the Kingdom of God had not yet arrived. Evidently, Christ was not referring to the universal Kingdom aspect of the Kingdom of God in His statement and teaching on prayer.

However, since the theocratic Kingdom ceased to exist after the fall of man, that aspect of the Kingdom was not present when Christ said, "the kingdom of God is at hand." Thus it is the theocratic Kingdom of God that corresponds to what Christ's statement indicated—that there was some sense in which the Kingdom was not yet present.

The same holds true with regard to Christ's model for prayer. He taught His disciples to pray for God's Kingdom to come in the future. The theocratic Kingdom of God will exist again during the future Millennium when Christ Himself will reign for 1,000 years. It will be the last phase of God's universal Kingdom-rule over this present earth. Thus the theocratic Kingdom aspect of the Kingdom of God matches the sense of the Kingdom of God involved in the prayer that Christ taught.

In both instances, therefore, Christ was referring to the future theocratic Kingdom of God, not to the universal Kingdom. Clearly, He indicated that the theocratic Kingdom of God was not yet present but will be in the future.

Meaning of Christ's Reference

Since Christ referred to the future theocratic Kingdom of God in His statement and model for prayer, what did He mean when He indicated that the Kingdom was "at hand"?

Normally, when people say that something is "at hand," they mean that it is near. Consequently, when Christ said, "the kingdom of God is at hand," He indicated that there was some sense in which the future theocratic Kingdom of God was near while He was present on earth. In fact, the word translated "is at hand" means "approach, come near,"[1] and the tense indicates that Christ was saying, "The kingdom of God has come near." But in what sense was it near then?

It was near in the sense of its potential for establishment in the world. Because Jesus Christ, who possessed the power necessary to establish the future theocratic Kingdom of God, was present on earth, that Kingdom had the potential to be established while He was here. That is what Christ meant when He said, "The kingdom of God is at hand"; and that is why He taught His disciples to pray, "Thy kingdom come."

Requirements for the Kingdom

What is required before the theocratic Kingdom of God can be reestablished in the world? John the Baptist (Mt. 3:1–2), Jesus Christ (Mt. 4:17; Mk. 1:15), and the apostles of Christ (Mt. 10:1–3, 7) all declared that the future theocratic

Kingdom was "at hand." Their message also referred to that Kingdom both as "the kingdom of heaven" and the "kingdom of God."

But the fact that both versions of the message are designated "the gospel of the kingdom" (Mt. 4:17, 23; Mk. 1:14–15) indicates that both referred to the same Kingdom. Thus John the Baptist, Christ, and His apostles all indicated that the future theocratic Kingdom of God was near in the sense of its potential for establishment in the world while Christ was present on earth.

Yet the gospel of the Kingdom included more than the declaration that the future theocratic Kingdom was near. It also included a twofold command for its hearers: They were to *believe* that it was near ("believe the gospel" [Mk. 1:15]), and they were to *repent* because that Kingdom was near ("Repent; for the kingdom of heaven is at hand" [Mt. 3:2; 4:17]).

The declaration that the Kingdom was at hand, combined with the command to believe and repent, implied that the theocratic Kingdom would not be established until the hearers of that gospel obeyed its twofold directive. In other words, the Kingdom would not be established until the hearers believed in the content of that gospel and repented.

DISTINCTIONS RELATED TO THE GOSPEL OF THE KINGDOM

The New Testament contains two different gospel messages: the gospel of the Kingdom and the gospel concerning Christ. The apostle Paul defined the latter in 1 Corinthians 15:1–5. Three distinctions reveal that they are not the same message.

Distinction in Content

The gospel of the Kingdom and the gospel concerning Christ were different in content. Whereas 1 Corinthians 15 spoke of the death, burial, and resurrection of Jesus Christ, the gospel of the Kingdom said nothing about those happenings. Three things support this distinction.

First, the record of Jesus sending His apostles to preach the gospel of the Kingdom is found in Matthew: "These twelve Jesus sent forth, and commanded them, saying, . . . And as ye go, preach, saying, The kingdom of heaven is at hand" (10:5, 7). Jesus did not include His coming death, burial, and resurrection in the content of that message.

Second, Matthew verified that fact when he recorded a change that happened after the apostles had been preaching the gospel of the Kingdom for some time: "From that time forth began Jesus to show unto his disciples, how he must go unto Jerusalem, and suffer many things from the elders and chief priests and scribes, and be killed, and be raised again the third day" (16:21). The language indicates that although the apostles had already been preaching the gospel of the Kingdom, Jesus had never told them about His coming death, burial, and resurrection. Thus the apostles had not been proclaiming those happenings while they were preaching the gospel of the Kingdom.

Third, Peter's negative reaction to that new revelation from Jesus demonstrated that the gospel of the Kingdom, which he had been preaching for some time, said nothing about Christ's death, burial, and resurrection: "Then Peter took him, and began to rebuke him, saying, Be it far from thee, Lord; this shall not be unto thee" (Mt. 16:22). If Peter had already been preaching Jesus' death, burial, and resurrection, he would not have reacted so strongly to Christ's revelation of it.

The fact is that the apostle Paul defined a second gospel in 1 Corinthians 15:1–5 when he wrote,

Moreover, brethren, I declare unto you the gospel which I preached unto you, which also ye have received, and in which ye stand; By which also ye are saved, if ye keep in memory what I preached unto you. . . . For I delivered unto you first of all that which I also received, that Christ died for our sins according to the scriptures; And that he was buried, and that he rose again the third day according to the scriptures; And that he was seen.

In contrast with the gospel of the Kingdom, this gospel that Paul preached and defined focused on Christ's death, burial, and resurrection. It said nothing about the Kingdom of God being at hand.

Distinction in Commission

The gospel of the Kingdom and the gospel concerning Christ also had distinct commissions associated with them. When Christ sent the apostles to preach the gospel of the Kingdom, He gave them a *restricted commission*. He said, "Go not into the way of the Gentiles, and into any city of the Samaritans enter not; But go, rather, to the lost sheep of the house of Israel. And as ye go, preach, saying, The kingdom of heaven is at hand" (Mt. 10:5–7).

In contrast, after Christ died and rose from the dead, He gave the apostles a *universal commission*. He said, "Go ye into all the world, and preach the gospel to every creature" (Mk. 16:15); and "Go ye, therefore, and teach all nations" (Mt. 28:19). This universal commission was associated with the gospel concerning Christ because Paul signified that the gospel he preached focused on Christ's crucifixion and "is the power of God unto salvation to everyone that believeth," whether Jew or Gentile (Rom. 1:16; cf. 1 Cor. 1:23–24).

Distinction in Preparation for Ministry

The third distinction is that these two gospels had different preparations for ministry associated with them. When Christ commissioned the apostles to preach the gospel of the Kingdom only to Israel, He ordered them not to take extra provisions for their ministry (Mt. 10:9–10). In contrast, when it became obvious that Israel would reject Christ and His gospel of the Kingdom and the gospel of 1 Corinthians 15 would become reality, Jesus commanded the apostles to take extra provisions for ministry (Lk. 22:35–36).

REASONS FOR THESE DISTINCTIONS

There are three main reasons for the distinctions between the two gospels.

Content

Why did John the Baptist and Christ preach a gospel that declared "the kingdom of God is at hand" but said nothing about Christ's death, burial, and resurrection? Why did Christ send His apostles to preach that distinct gospel? Four items shed light on the reason.

First, the primary purpose of Christ's miracles was to demonstrate He was the promised Messiah who could establish the theocratic Kingdom and its prophesied transformation of nature. Those miracles supported the gospel-of-the-Kingdom message that the theocratic Kingdom was near in the sense of its potential for establishment. It was near because the Messiah, Jesus, who possessed the power necessary to establish that Kingdom, was present.

Second, John the Baptist (Mt. 3:1–2), Jesus Christ (Mt. 4:17; Mk. 1:15), and the apostles (Mt. 10:1–3, 7) all implied that the hearers of that gospel must fulfill two requirements for the theocratic Kingdom to be established: (1) they must believe the gospel's declaration that the theocratic Kingdom was near, in the sense of its potential for establishment (Mk. 1:14–15). This faith would involve

175

belief that Jesus was the Messiah who had the power necessary to establish the Kingdom. (2) They must repent (Mt. 3:2; 4:17, 23).

Third, through His triumphal entry into Jerusalem on a donkey's colt, Jesus officially presented Himself to Israel as its Messiah Prince—the one who, as King, would administer God's rule over all the earth in the theocratic Kingdom (Lk. 19:29–40). He thereby fulfilled Zechariah 9:9, which foretold that this was how Jerusalem's King would come (Mt. 21:4–5).

Fourth, on the day of His triumphal entry, Jesus wept over the city and said, "If thou hadst known, even thou, at least in this thy day, the things which belong unto thy peace! But now they are hidden from thine eyes" (Lk. 19:42). Then He warned Jerusalem that the city and its inhabitants would later be destroyed by an enemy "because thou knewest not the time of thy visitation" (Lk. 19:44).

Christ's weeping and His statements indicated the incredible significance that specific day had for Jerusalem and its inhabitants. The word translated "time" in the expression *the time of thy visitation* connoted the basic sense of the "fateful and decisive point" in time.[2] It implied that that point in time was "ordained by God" and, if people missed its significance and did not act accordingly, there could be "no second chance."[3] The word translated "known" and "knewest" in Christ's statements referred to "acknowledgment, and obedient or grateful submission to what is known."[4]

In light of these meanings, Christ was saying that the day of His triumphal entry into Jerusalem was the fateful and decisive point in time ordained by God for the capital of the nation and its inhabitants. It was the point in time that would determine their fate. For more than three years, the gospel of the Kingdom had been preached to the nation, and many miracles had substantiated the truthfulness of that message. Now, on the day of His triumphal entry, Christ officially presented Himself to the nation as its Messiah Prince in the exact manner that Israel's Scriptures had indicated the Messiah could be identified (Zech. 9:9). In addition, Jesus did so on the exact day that Scripture foretold the Messiah would present Himself (Dan. 9:24–25).

In light of this knowledge, the time had come for the nation, through its governing rulers in the capital city, to make a fateful, decisive decision. Would it acknowledge the truth that the future theocratic Kingdom was near in the sense of its potential for establishment and that Jesus was the Messiah who had the power necessary to establish the Kingdom? Would it render obedient or grateful submission to that acknowledged truth by repenting?

If, on that day, it would fulfill both these requirements, it would enjoy a future of peace because the theocratic Kingdom would be established. Failure to fulfill these requirements on that day, however, would mean the nation would suffer future destruction because God would withhold the establishment of the theocratic Kingdom.

Together, these four factors reveal the reason for preaching the distinct gospel of the Kingdom. It was Christ's way of offering the future theocratic Kingdom to Israel and telling the nation the requirements for its establishment at that time.

Commission

When Christ sent the apostles to preach the gospel of the Kingdom, why did He give them a restricted commission? Why were they to preach the gospel of the Kingdom exclusively to the people of Israel, not to the Samaritans or Gentiles? The reason was that God had determined that the theocratic Kingdom not be established until Israel acknowledges the true Messiah and repents (Zech. 12—14; Acts 3:12-21).

But why must Israel—but not Samaritans and Gentiles—do so before the establishment of the theocratic Kingdom? The Old Testament reveals the reason. When God established a unique covenant relationship with Israel at Sinai, He signified His ordained purpose for that nation: "Ye shall be unto me a kingdom of priests, and an holy nation" (Ex. 19:6). In ancient times, Israel's priests were to be spiritual leaders, helping the people maintain a right relationship with God. Thus God had designated the nation of Israel, not Samaritans or Gentiles, to be the spiritual leader of the world, helping all other peoples maintain right relationships with Him.

Tragically, because of its own spiritual failure, Israel has not yet fulfilled that purpose. But other Old Testament passages foretell that it will in the future theocratic Kingdom. For example, Isaiah 61:6 declares that in the future, the people of Israel "shall be named the Priests of the LORD; men shall call you the Ministers of our God." Zechariah 8:22-23 states,

> Yea, many peoples and strong nations shall come to seek the LORD of hosts in Jerusalem, and to pray before the LORD. Thus saith the LORD of hosts: In those days it shall come to pass that ten men shall take hold out of all languages of the nations, even shall take hold of the skirt of him that is a Jew, saying, We will go with you; for we have heard that God is with you.

In addition, Isaiah 2:1–3 and Micah 4:1–2 indicate that "in the last days" Jerusalem will become the spiritual center of the world. Many nations will come there to be taught God's ways, "for the law shall go forth from Zion, and the word of the LORD from Jerusalem" (Mic. 4:2).

For Israel to be the spiritual leader of the world in the future theocratic Kingdom, Israel itself must come into right relationship with God. That is why God will not establish the theocratic Kingdom until Israel acknowledges the true Messiah and repents. And that is the reason Christ commissioned the apostles to preach the gospel of the Kingdom only to Israel.

Preparation for Ministry

When Christ sent the apostles to preach the gospel of the Kingdom, why did He forbid them to take extra provisions for their itinerant ministry? Why did He command them to do what was contrary to the practice of those whose work required them to travel from place to place over long periods of time? In Matthew 10:10, Christ told them why: "for the workman is worthy of his food." His point was that He was sending them out as representatives of Himself and His Kingdom message. Thus their daily food would be provided in a manner fitting His claim to be the Messiah and His message that the theocratic Kingdom of God was at hand.

The Old Testament prophets foretold that, when the Messiah will establish and rule over the future theocratic Kingdom, He will bless the earth with a superabundance of food. The daily provision of the apostles' food, contrary to the normal practice of storing extra provisions, would support the truthfulness of Jesus' Messianic claim and His gospel of the Kingdom.

CONCLUSION

These three distinctions show that, through the preaching of the gospel of the Kingdom and the supporting miracles, Christ offered the future theocratic Kingdom to the nation of Israel. Israel's response is also recorded in Scripture and will be examined in the next chapter.

CHAPTER TWENTY-TWO

ISRAEL'S RESPONSE TO JESUS CHRIST AND HIS OFFER OF THE KINGDOM

C hrist offered the future theocratic Kingdom to Israel and told the nation what it must do for the Kingdom to be established. He offered the Kingdom through the preaching of the gospel of the Kingdom and the performance of miracles verifying that message. This chapter examines Israel's response to Jesus Christ and His offer of the Kingdom.

ISRAEL'S RESPONSE FORETOLD
Old Testament Prophecies

Through Israel's Old Testament Scriptures, God foretold that the nation would reject the Messiah and His message. More than 700 years before Christ preached the gospel of the Kingdom to Israel and demonstrated the truthfulness of that message through His powerful miracles, God moved Israel's prophet Isaiah to write, "Who hath believed our report? And to whom is the arm of the Lord revealed?" (Is. 53:1). This prophecy foretold that the people of Israel would not believe the report that the Messiah was present or the subsequent truth that the theocratic Kingdom of God was at hand in the sense of its potential for establishment.

In the Bible, "the arm of the Lord" refers to God's mighty power (Ps. 89:10, 13; Is. 62:8; Jer. 32:17). In Isaiah 53:1 that expression refers specifically to God's revelation to Israel of His mighty power through the miracles that Christ performed in conjunction with the preaching of the gospel of the Kingdom. Thus, through the prophet Isaiah, God foretold that, in spite of the display of God's mighty power through the miracles that Christ would perform, the people of Israel would believe neither the report that He was the Messiah nor the fact that the theocratic Kingdom of God was at hand. Several years after Israel rejected Christ and His offer of the Kingdom, the apostle John confirmed this understanding of Isaiah 53:1. John wrote,

But though he had done so many miracles before them, yet they believed not on him; That the saying of Isaiah, the prophet, might be fulfilled, which he spoke, Lord, who hath believed our report? And to whom hath the arm of the Lord been revealed? (Jn. 12:37–38).

Through the Isaiah 53 prophecy, God foretold that Israel would not desire or esteem the Messiah when He would come. In fact, He would be rejected (vv. 2–3).

God indicated further that He would use this rejection as His means of effecting the death of the Messiah as an offering for the sins, transgressions, and iniquities of the people (vv. 5–6, 8, 10–12). One reason why His death would be necessary was that, just as sheep wander from their shepherd, so the people of Israel had strayed from God by turning to their own way instead of following Him. Thus their iniquity had to be laid on the Messiah (v. 6).

More than 500 years before Christ offered the theocratic Kingdom to Israel, God delivered a significant prophecy to Israel's prophet Daniel through the angel Gabriel. Gabriel indicated that this prophecy related specifically to Daniel's people and their holy city, Jerusalem (Dan. 9:24). God revealed the exact time the Messiah would officially present Himself to Israel as its prince (the one who could establish the theocratic Kingdom and rule over it as king, Dan. 9:25). Jesus Christ fulfilled this prophecy through His triumphal entry into Jerusalem on the foal of a donkey (Mt. 21:1–5). Centuries earlier, God had revealed that this was precisely how Israel's future King would present Himself to the nation (Zech. 9:9).

Then God indicated that, after Messiah's official presentation, He would be "cut off" with a violent death (Dan. 9:26). Christ was crucified several days after His triumphal entry (Mt. 27:33–50). This portion of Daniel's prophecy implied that Israel would reject the Messiah and His offer of the theocratic Kingdom.

The prophecy also revealed that, after the Messiah would be cut off, Jerusalem and the second Temple would be destroyed by a particular people (Dan. 9:26). Christ also foretold this future destruction, indicating it would occur because the nation did not recognize the significance of the day of His triumphal entry and the peace that was available through His offer of the theocratic Kingdom (Mt. 24:1–2; Lk. 19:41–44). The Romans were the people who fulfilled these prophecies. They destroyed Jerusalem and the second Temple in A.D. 70.

Jesus Christ's Prophecies

While Christ was present on earth, He Himself foretold His future rejection and death. After His 12 disciples had preached the gospel of the Kingdom to Israel for a significant time, Jesus began to tell them "how he must go unto Jerusalem, and suffer many things from the elders and chief priests and scribes, and be killed, and be raised again the third day" (Mt. 16:21). Later Jesus told the disciples, "The Son of man shall be betrayed into the hands of men, And they shall kill him, and the third day he shall be raised again" (Mt. 17:22–23). On His last journey to Jerusalem before His death, Christ spoke these words to them:

Behold, we go up to Jerusalem; and the Son of man shall be betrayed unto the chief priests and unto the scribes, and they shall condemn him to death, And shall deliver him to the Gentiles to mock, and to scourge, and to crucify him. And the third day he shall rise again (Mt. 20:18–19).

Christ clearly asserted that His rejection, death, and resurrection had all been foretold in the Old Testament writings of Israel's prophets (Lk. 18:31).

In Matthew 21:33–40 Jesus taught a parable about vineyard husbandmen who killed the vineyard owner's son when his father sent him to the vineyard to collect its fruit. In this parable the owner of the vineyard represented God the Father; the owner's son represented God's Son, Jesus Christ; and the husbandmen represented Israel's religious leaders. Through this parable Christ foretold that the religious leaders would reject Him and His offer of the theocratic Kingdom and would have Him killed (v. 42). He also foretold the tragic consequence of that rejection: The theocratic Kingdom of God would not be given to the nation of Israel that existed at that time. Instead, it would be given to a future nation of Israel that would produce what God wants (v. 43).

SATAN'S ROLE IN ISRAEL'S RESPONSE

In the parable of the sower, Christ revealed that Satan played a key role in Israel's rejection of Him and His offer of the theocratic Kingdom. At the beginning of the parable, Jesus stated, "Behold, a sower went forth to sow; And when he sowed, some of the seeds fell by the wayside, and the fowls came and devoured them" (Mt. 13:3–4). In His interpretation of the parable, Christ indicated that the seeds represented the message concerning the theocratic Kingdom and the birds represented Satan. He said,

Hear, therefore, the parable of the sower. When any one heareth the word of the kingdom, and understandeth it not, then cometh the wicked one, and catcheth away that which was sown in his heart. This is he which received seed by the wayside (vv. 18–19).

Christ thereby revealed that as He and others were preaching the gospel of the Kingdom to the people of Israel, Satan followed behind them and snatched that message away from many of the hearers, so they would not believe it and repent.

Satan did so because of the following biblical truth: Christ will crush Satan and his kingdom, remove them totally from the earth, and establish God's theocratic Kingdom when Israel believes the gospel of the Kingdom and repents (Zech. 12—14; Rev. 19:11—20:6; Acts 3:19–21). In light of that truth, the preaching of the gospel of the Kingdom to Israel and the performance of the miracles that supported the truthfulness of that message posed a serious threat to Satan and his domain. Thus, to prevent Christ from crushing and removing him and his kingdom when He was here, Satan worked to prevent the people of Israel from believing the gospel of the Kingdom and repenting.

ISRAEL'S RESPONSE FULFILLED

The religious leaders of the nation played the key role in the rejection of Jesus Christ and His offer of the theocratic Kingdom. They were displeased with His miracles, His cleansing of the Temple, and the people's response to His ministry (Mt. 21:15; Mk. 11:18). They challenged His authority and planned how they could take and kill Him (Mt. 21:23; 26:3–5). They paid money for His betrayal, sent a large multitude to take Him, sought false witness against Him, and pronounced Him guilty of death (Mt. 26:14–15, 47, 59, 66). After more deliberation, they sent Him to

Pilate, accused Him before Pilate and Herod, and persuaded a multitude to press Pilate to execute Him (Mt. 27:1–2, 12, 20).

THE "WHAT IF" QUESTION

Some people ask the question, "What if Israel had believed the gospel of the Kingdom and repented when Jesus Christ was here? Would that have jeopardized the necessity of Christ dying for the sins of the world and, therefore, the salvation of human beings?"

First, the fact that both the Old Testament and Christ Himself foretold Israel's rejection of Him and His offer of the theocratic Kingdom and His death indicates that these rejections and His death were certainties. Second, even if Israel had believed the gospel of the Kingdom and repented, Christ would have died for the sins of the world.

If Israel had believed and repented, the nation would have acclaimed Christ as its King. The Roman government would have regarded this action as the beginning of a revolt and undoubtedly would have crucified Him. Then Christ would have risen from the dead, crushed and removed Satan and his kingdom (including the Roman Empire), and established God's theocratic Kingdom on the earth.

The Israel of Moses' day did not enter the Promised Land of Canaan because of unbelief. Thus its entrance was postponed for 40 years until the nation of Joshua's day believed God's promise. Similarly, the nation of Israel of Christ's First Coming did not receive the promised theocratic Kingdom because of unbelief. It did not believe His message and the witness of His miracles. Thus God postponed the establishment of that Kingdom until Christ's Second Coming when the nation of Israel of that day will believe.

EVIDENCES OF THE POSTPONEMENT

We have the following biblical evidences of God's postponement of His Kingdom.

Jesus Christ and the Throne of David

Biblical Declarations. Isaiah prophesied concerning the Messiah:
Of the increase of his government and peace there shall be no end, upon the throne of David, and upon his kingdom, to order it, and to establish it with justice and with righteousness from henceforth even forever (Isa. 9:7).

The angel Gabriel announced that God will give Jesus Christ the throne of His ancestor David, Jesus will reign over the house of Jacob forever, and Jesus' Kingdom will never end (Lk. 1:31–33).

The apostle Peter declared that God had sworn with an oath to David "that of the fruit of his loins, according to the flesh, he would raise up Christ to sit on his throne" (Acts 2:30).

These biblical declarations indicate that Christ's Kingdom (the future theocratic Kingdom) will be present and functioning when He sits on David's throne. They thereby imply that the future theocratic Kingdom will be established when Jesus Christ takes His seat on David's throne. In light of this implication, to determine the time of the theocratic Kingdom's establishment, we must discern the time of Christ's taking His seat on David's throne.

Did Christ do so when He ascended to heaven after His resurrection and sat on the right hand of God and God's throne (Mk. 16:19; Heb. 12:2)? Advocates of Covenant Theology and Progressive Dispensationalism claim that, at that time, Christ took His seat on David's throne. If so, then David's throne is to be equated with God's throne in heaven; and there is some sense in which the theocratic Kingdom was established at that time.

Or will Christ take His seat on David's throne in conjunction with His Second Coming to earth after the Great Tribulation (Mt. 24:29–31)? If He will do so at that future time, then David's throne is separate and distinct from God's throne in heaven; and no part of the theocratic Kingdom has been or will be established until Christ's Second Coming.

To determine which of these positions is correct, we must examine three biblical items.

Description of the Throne in Heaven. Three facts should be noted concerning the throne in heaven. First, the Scriptures consistently describe it as God's throne, indicating that it belongs to God the Father (Lam. 5:19; Mt. 5:34; 23:22; Acts 7:49; Heb. 8:1; 12:2; Rev. 7:15; 12:5; 14:5). Second, the Bible signifies that God's throne is located in the heavenly realm (Ps. 11:4; 103:19; Heb. 8:1). In fact, Scripture declares that heaven is God's throne (Isa. 66:1; Mt. 5:34; 23:22; Acts 7:49). Third, the Bible never calls God's throne in heaven "the throne of David."

Distinctiveness of the Throne of David. Several factors indicate that David's throne is separate and distinct from God's throne in heaven.

First, several descendants of David have sat on his throne, but only one of his descendants ever sits on the right hand of God's throne. That descendant is Jesus Christ (Ps. 110:1; Heb. 8:1; 12:2).

Second, David's throne was not established before his lifetime (2 Sam. 7:16–17). By contrast, since God has always ruled over His creation, His throne in heaven was established long before David's throne (Ps. 93:1–2).

Third, since God's throne was established long before David's and God's was established forever (Lam. 5:19), then it was not necessary for God to promise to establish David's throne forever (2 Sam. 7:16) if they are the same throne.

Fourth, David's throne was on earth, not in heaven. David and his descendants who sat on his throne exercised an earthly ruling authority. They never exercised ruling authority in or from heaven. By contrast, as noted earlier, the Bible indicates that God's throne is in heaven.

Fifth, the Bible's consistent description of David's throne indicates that it belongs to David. When God talked to David about his throne, God referred to it as "thy throne" (2 Sam. 7:16; Ps. 89:4; 132:12). When God mentioned David's throne to others, He referred to it as "his throne" (Ps. 89:29, 36; Jer. 33:21), "David's throne" (Jer. 13:13), and "the throne of David" (Jer. 17:25; 22:2, 4, 30). By contrast, the Scriptures' consistent description of the throne in heaven indicates that it belongs to God the Father.

Distinctiveness of Christ's Throne. Several things indicate that, when the future theocratic Kingdom is established and Jesus rules over it, the throne on which He sits is separate and distinct from God's throne in heaven.

First, several decades after Christ ascended to heaven, He made the following statement in Revelation 3:21: "To him that overcometh will I grant to sit with me in my throne, even as I also overcame, and am set down with my Father in his throne." Christ drew a clear distinction between His throne (where He and His overcomers will sit in the future) and God's (where He presently sits with His Father).

Second, God the Father's declaration to His Son, Jesus Christ, "Thy throne, O God, is forever and ever" (Ps. 45:6; Heb. 1:8) indicates that God recognizes a throne that belongs to Christ, separate and distinct from His own.

These distinctions by Christ and God militate against Christ's throne and God's throne in heaven being the same. Since it is the throne of David that God promised to give to Christ (Lk. 1:31–32), then Christ's throne must be David's throne. And since Christ's throne is separate and distinct from God's throne in heaven, then David's throne must be separate and distinct from God's throne in heaven.

Conclusion. In light of the description of the throne in heaven, the distinctiveness of David's throne, and the distinctiveness of Christ's throne, we can draw the following conclusions. First, David's throne is not equatable with God's throne in heaven. Second, since that is true, when Christ ascended to heaven after His resurrection, He did not take His seat on David's throne. Instead, He sat down on the right hand of God's throne.

Third, the fact that Christ has continued to sit on the right hand of God's throne in heaven to this present time indicates He has not yet taken His seat on David's throne. Fourth, since the future theocratic Kingdom will be established when Christ takes His seat on David's throne and, since He has not yet done so, then no part of the theocratic Kingdom has been established yet.

Jesus Christ and the Sealed Scroll

In chapter 16, I examined the relationship of Christ to the sealed scroll of Revelation 5, noting the following truths: As a result of the first Adam joining Satan's revolt against God, mankind temporarily lost its God-given tenant possession of the earth. In addition, the original theocratic Kingdom of God was lost from the earth. Satan usurped the rule of the world system away from God and has continued to dominate it ever since. To fulfill His purpose for history, God must crush Satan by ridding the earth of him and his world-system rule; and then He must restore His theocratic Kingdom-rule to this earth before its history ends.

God revealed that Jesus Christ, as the last Adam and mankind's Kinsman-Redeemer, would do the following: (1) Redeem mankind's lost tenant possession of the earth, (2) crush Satan, and (3) establish the future theocratic Kingdom (when tenant possession will be restored to mankind).

Through the shedding of His blood on the cross, Christ paid the price to redeem mankind's inheritance of the earth. At that time, a scroll deed of purchase for that inheritance was made. The scroll was legal evidence that Christ paid the redemption price and, therefore, has the right to do two things—rid the earth of Satan and his world-system rule and establish the future theocratic Kingdom.

The scroll was sealed with seven seals and placed in God's right hand in heaven (Rev. 5:1, 7). This sealing and placement were to make the content of the scroll secure from tampering. This security was necessary because Christ neither rid the earth of Satan and his world-system rule nor established the theocratic Kingdom immediately after He had paid the redemption price at the cross. Instead, He ascended from earth to heaven (Acts 1:9–11); and there He has remained at the right hand of God and God's throne ever since.

It was imperative that the content of the scroll deed of purchase be kept secure from tampering during Christ's long absence from the earth; so when He returns, it can provide legal evidence of His right to rid the earth of Satan and his rule and establish the theocratic Kingdom. Christ will have taken the scroll from God's hand and broken its seven seals by the time of His future coming, so He can read its content publicly at that time as evidence of His right (Rev. 5:1—6:17; 8:1). Not until then will Christ rid the earth of Satan and his rule and establish the future theocratic Kingdom.

This relationship of Jesus Christ to the sealed scroll of Revelation 5 indicates that (1) Christ did not establish the theocratic Kingdom of God after He ascended to heaven and sat at the right hand of God and God's throne, and (2) He will not establish it until His Second Coming to earth.

Chronology of Matthew 24—25

In Matthew 24—25, Christ presented a chronological order of future events related to His Second Coming. In Matthew 24:29–31 He taught that, after the Great Tribulation, He will come as the Son of man in the clouds of heaven with power and great glory and with His angels.

Matthew 25:31 refers to the same time as Matthew 24:30–31, namely, the coming of the Son of man in glory with the holy angels. Jesus declared that, at that time, the Son of man will "sit upon the throne of his glory" (Mt. 25:31, David's throne as noted earlier); will reign as King; and will send righteous people into the theocratic Kingdom (v. 34).

Through this chronological order, Christ revealed that He will not take His seat on David's throne, reign as King, and send people into the promised Kingdom of God until He returns after the Great Tribulation. He thereby indicated that the theocratic Kingdom will not be established until His Second Coming.

Order of Events at Christ's Second Coming

In His parable of the tares, Christ taught the following order of events at His Second Coming: All the unsaved, meaning those who have not received Christ as Savior (the tares, "the children of the wicked one," Mt. 13:38–39), who are living on the earth at His Second Coming ("the end of the age," v. 39) will be removed from the earth in judgment by the angels of the Son of man (vv. 40–42). Then all the saved (the good seed, "the children of the kingdom," v. 38) living on earth at Christ's Second Coming will remain there to enter the theocratic Kingdom (v. 43).

Christ taught the same order of events in His parable of the dragnet. At His Second Coming ("the end of the age," Mt. 13:49), "the angels shall come forth, and separate the wicked from among the righteous, And shall cast them into the furnace of fire; there shall be wailing and gnashing of teeth" (vv. 49–50).

Jesus presented this same order again in Matthew 24:37–41. There He taught that the order of events at His Second Coming after the Great Tribulation will be the same as the order of events in Noah's day (v. 37). Back then the flood took all the living unsaved from the earth in judgment while all the saved (Noah and his family) remained to enter the next period of history (vv. 38–39). After relating this sequence, Jesus said, "so shall also the coming of the Son of man be" (v. 39). At His Second Coming after the Great Tribulation, the living unsaved will be "taken" from the earth in judgment; and the living saved will be "left" on the earth to enter the next period of history, the theocratic Kingdom Age (vv. 40–41).

Through these teachings Christ indicated that at His Second Coming all living unsaved people will be removed from earth in judgment before the future theocratic Kingdom will be established. The fact that all unsaved people have not yet been removed in judgment prompts the conclusion that the theocratic Kingdom has not yet begun.

Parable of Luke 19:12–27

As Jesus drew near to Jerusalem shortly before His death, He spoke a parable to His disciples "because they thought that the kingdom of God should immediately appear" (Lk. 19:11). Christ talked about a nobleman who travelled a long distance "to receive for himself a kingdom, and to return" (v. 12). Because this journey required the nobleman to be away for an extended time, he entrusted portions of his wealth as stewardships to his servants. He ordered his servants to tend his wealth for his benefit until he returned to establish the kingdom he would receive while away. When he returned, he gave ruling positions in the government of his kingdom to the servants who had exercised their stewardships faithfully for his gain (vv. 13–24).

The nobleman in the parable represented Jesus Christ. Jesus was indicating to the disciples that He would go away to a faraway place (heaven) for an extended time to receive the future theocratic Kingdom. When He had it, He would return to earth to establish it. Thus the theocratic Kingdom of God would not be established immediately but would be postponed until His Second Coming.

Daniel 7 Prophecy

Two parts of the prophecy recorded in Daniel 7:9–27 also signify that the Kingdom will not be established until the Second Coming. First, in verses 9–14, Daniel saw God the Father (the Ancient of days) give the Messiah the following:

And there was given him dominion, and glory, and a kingdom, that all people, nations, and languages should serve him; his dominion is an everlasting dominion, which shall not pass away, and his kingdom that which shall not be destroyed (v. 14).

Verse 13 revealed that the Messiah would receive His kingdom (the theocratic Kingdom) in conjunction with His coming as the Son of man with the clouds of heaven.

Christ indicated that this part of this prophecy will be fulfilled when He, as the Son of man, will come in the clouds of heaven after the end of the Great Tribulation (Mt. 24:29–30). Not until then, therefore, will He receive the theocratic Kingdom to establish it.

Second, the part of this prophecy recorded in verses 21–22 and 25–27 revealed that the future theocratic Kingdom will not be established until the Antichrist (the little horn who will war against the saints) has been judged and his dominion taken away and destroyed. Since the judgment of the Antichrist and his dominion has not yet occurred, we must conclude that the theocratic Kingdom has not yet been established.

Revelation 19:11–21 signifies that the Antichrist will not be judged and his dominion taken away and destroyed until the Second Coming of Jesus Christ. Thus the theocratic Kingdom will not be established until the Second Coming.

Israel's Repentance

Earlier I noted that the future theocratic Kingdom will not be established until the nation of Israel believes the gospel of the Kingdom and repents of its unbelief and rebellion against God and His Messiah. Neither of those events has occurred yet. As a result, the theocratic Kingdom has not yet been established.

Israel's prophet Zechariah foretold the following events:

- When the armies of all the nations of the world come against Jerusalem, the Messiah will come out of heaven (Zech. 12:2–3, 9–10).
- At that time the people of Israel will see Him and the wounds of His crucifixion in His resurrected body (12:10).
- They will recognize that the one who was rejected and crucified in His First Coming was their true Messiah, and they will repent (change their minds concerning Him to the point of trusting Him as their Messiah and Savior, 12:10–14).
- In response to their repentance, God will cleanse them of their sin (13:1); and the Messiah will destroy the armies that have come against Jerusalem (14:3, 12–15).
- Then Christ will reign as King over all the earth (14:9).

These Scriptures indicate that the theocratic Kingdom will not be established until Israel repents in conjunction with Christ's Second Coming.

Restoration of Nature

In chapter 19, I noted that Christ taught that nature will be restored to its prefall condition when He, as the Son of man, "shall sit on the throne of his glory" and the apostles "shall sit upon twelve thrones, judging the twelve tribes of Israel" (Mt. 19:28). In Luke 22:28–30, Christ revealed that the apostles will "sit on thrones judging the twelve tribes of Israel" in His "kingdom." Together these passages indicate that the restoration of nature will not take place until Christ and the apostles sit on thrones to rule the world in the future theocratic Kingdom.

The fact that nature has not yet been restored to its prefall condition prompts the conclusions that Christ presently is not seated on the throne of His glory; and, therefore, the theocratic Kingdom has not yet been established.

A comparison of Matthew 25:31 with 24:29–31 indicates that Christ will not sit on the "throne of his glory" until His Second Coming after the Great Tribulation. Thus the theocratic Kingdom will not be established until His Second Coming after the Great Tribulation.

Chronological Order of Revelation

The book of Revelation presents the following order of events: (1) Christ's Second Coming to earth to destroy the political and military forces of Satan's domain (19:11–21), (2) the imprisonment of Satan in the bottomless pit for 1,000 years (20:1–3), and (3) the theocratic Kingdom reign of Christ for 1,000 years (20:4–6). Two facts should be noted in light of this order.

First, this order indicates that the theocratic Kingdom will not be established until Satan and his rule of the world system have been removed from the earth. It is evident that Satan and his rule were not removed while Christ was on earth in His First Coming or when He sat down at the right hand of God in heaven because of the following two facts. Years after Christ ascended to heaven, Paul taught that Satan was still "the god of this age" (2 Cor. 4:4); and John declared that the whole world was still lying under the control of "the wicked one" (literal translation of 1 Jn. 5:19). Thus the theocratic Kingdom was not established during Christ's First Coming or when He sat down at God's right hand in heaven.

Second, this order in Revelation indicates that the theocratic Kingdom will not be established until the Second Coming of Christ.

CONCLUSION

The evidences presented in this chapter consistently prompt the same conclusion: The theocratic Kingdom of God is yet to come. It was not established with the nation of Israel of Christ's First Coming. Instead, its establishment has been postponed until His Second Coming.

We have much to look forward to when Christ comes again!

ENDNOTES

Introduction

1 D. A. Kidd, "doctrina," *Collins Latin Gem Dictionary,* Collins, London, 1957, p. 109.

2 "Doctrine," *Webster's New International Dictionary of the English Language,* 2nd ed., 1939, p. 763.

3 Walter Grundmann, "proskartereo," *Theological Dictionary of the New Testament,* Vol. III, Wm. B. Eerdmans Publishing Co., Grand Rapids, 1965, p. 618.

4 Ibid., p. 619.

Chapter 1

1 Bruce K. Waltke, "galah," *Theological Wordbook of the Old Testament,* Vol. I, Moody Press, Chicago, 1980, pp. 350–351.

2 Albrecht Oepke, "apocalupto," *Theological Dictionary of the New Testament,* Vol. III, Wm. B. Eerdmans Publishing Co., Grand Rapids, 1965, p. 591.

3 William F. Arndt and F. Wilbur Gingrich, "apocalupto," *A Greek-English Lexicon of the New Testament,* The University of Chicago Press, Chicago, 1957, p. 91.

4 Oepke, p. 574.

5 Ibid., p. 583.

6 Arndt and Gingrich, "musterion," p. 532.

7 Arndt and Gingrich, "anabaino," p. 50.

8 G. Bornkamm, "musterion," *Theological Dictionary of the New Testament,* Vol. IV, Wm. B. Eerdmans Publishing Co., Grand Rapids, 1967, p. 820.

9 Ibid., pp. 820–821.

Chapter 2

1 John N. Oswalt, "kabod," *Theological Wordbook of the Old Testament,* Vol. I, Moody Press, Chicago, 1980, p. 426.

2 Ibid.

3 L. Koehler and W. Baumgartner, *Lexicon in Veteris Testamenti Libros,* 2nd ed., Eng.-Ger., 1958, quoted by Leonard J. Coppes, "nagad," *Theological Wordbook of the Old Testament,* Vol. II, Moody Press, Chicago, 1980, p. 549.

4 Sir James Jeans, *The Universe Around Us,* The University Press, Cambridge, 1960, p. 42.

5 Peter Lancaster Brown, *Astronomy in Color,* The Macmillan Company, New York, 1972, p. 43.

6 Jeans, p. 181.

7 Brown, p. 218.

8 Ibid.

9 Ibid.

10 Patrick Moore, *The Observer's Book of Astronomy,* Frederick Warne & Co., New York, 1962, p. 148.

11 *Science News,* January 14, 1995, pp. 20–21.

12 Leonard J. Coppes, "naba," *Theological Wordbook of the Old Testament,* Vol. II, Moody Press,

Chicago, 1980, p. 548.

[13] Earl S. Kalland, "milla," *Theological Wordbook of the Old Testament*, Vol. I, Moody Press, Chicago, 1980, p. 510.

[14] Ralph H. Alexander, "tebel," *Theological Wordbook of the Old Testament*, Vol. I, Moody Press, Chicago, 1980, p. 359.

[15] John E. Hartley, "gaw," *Theological Wordbook of the Old Testament*, Vol. II, Moody Press, Chicago, 1980, p. 791.

[16] "Marriage," *The Universal Jewish Encyclopedia*, Vol. 7, 1948, p. 373.

[17] "Huppah," *The Universal Jewish Encyclopedia*, Vol. 5, 1948, p. 504.

[18] "Solar energy," *The New Encyclopaedia Britannica*, Vol. 10, 1993, p. 941.

[19] "Sun," *The New Encyclopaedia Britannica*, Vol. 11, 1993, p. 387.

[20] "The Sun," *The New Encyclopaedia Britannica*, Vol. 27, 1993, p. 456.

[21] Rudolf Bultmann, "euphrosune," *Theological Dictionary of the New Testament*, Vol. II, Wm. B. Eerdmans Publishing Co., Grand Rapids, 1964, p. 774.

[22] William F. Arndt and F. Wilbur Gingrich, "asebeia," *A Greek-English Lexicon of the New Testament*, The University of Chicago Press, Chicago, 1957, p. 114.

[23] Gottlob Schrenk, "adikia," *Theological Dictionary of the New Testament*, Vol. I, Wm. B. Eerdmans Publishing Co., Grand Rapids, 1964, pp. 154, 156.

[24] Ibid.

[25] Arndt and Gingrich, "dokeo," p. 201.

[26] Arndt and Gingrich, "katecho," p. 423.

[27] Herman Hanse, "katecho," *Theological Dictionary of the New Testament*, Vol. II, Wm. B. Eerdmans Publishing Co., Grand Rapids, 1964, p. 829.

[28] Bultmann, "aletheia," Vol. I, p. 243.

[29] H. E. Dana and Julius R. Mantey, "en," *A Manual Grammar of the Greek New Testament*, The Macmillan Company, New York, 1927, p. 105.

[30] Dana and Mantey, "dioti," p. 245.

[31] Arndt and Gingrich, "gnostos," p. 163.

[32] Bultmann, "gnostos," Vol. I, p. 719.

[33] Arndt and Gingrich, "phaneros," p. 860.

[34] Rudolph Bultmann and Dieter Luhrmann, "phaneros," *Theological Dictionary of the New Testament*, Vol. IX, Wm. B. Eerdmans Publishing Co., Grand Rapids, 1974, p. 3.

[35] Ibid.

[36] Wilhelm Michaelis, "kathorao," *Theological Dictionary of the New Testament*, Vol. V, Wm. B. Eerdmans Publishing Co., Grand Rapids, 1967, p. 380.

[37] Arndt and Gingrich, "kathorao," p. 392.

[38] Arndt and Gingrich, "theiotes," p. 354.

[39] Hermann Kleinknecht, "theiotes," *Theological Dictionary of the New Testament*, Vol. III, Wm. B. Eerdmans Publishing Co., Grand Rapids, 1965, p. 123.

[40] W. E. Lunt, *History of England*, 3rd ed., Harper & Brothers, New York, 1945, pp. 349–350.

[41] Ibid., p. 350.

[42] Ibid.

[43] Walter Phelps Hall and Robert Greenhalgh Albion, *A History of England and the British Empire,* 3rd ed., Ginn and Company, Boston, 1953, p. 298.

[44] Earle E. Cairns, *Christianity Through the Centuries,* rev. ed., Zondervan Publishing House, Grand Rapids, 1981, p. 333.

[45] Lunt, p. 350.

[46] Ibid., p. 843.

[47] William L. Shirer, *The Rise and Fall of the Third Reich,* Fawcett Publications, Inc., Greenwich, Conn., 1962, p. 994.

[48] Ibid., pp. 994–995.

[49] Ibid., pp. 1086–1087.

[50] Ibid., p. 1087.

[51] Ibid., pp. 1080–1081.

[52] Ibid., p. 1088.

[53] Ibid., p. 1081.

Chapter 6

[1] William F. Arndt and F. Wilbur Gingrich, "dokeo," *A Greek-English Lexicon of the New Testament,* The University of Chicago Press, Chicago, 1957, p. 201.

[2] Arndt and Gingrich, "kathexes," p. 389.

[3] Arndt and Gingrich, "parakoloutheo," p. 624.

[4] Arndt and Gingrich, "akribos," p. 32.

[5] Leon Morris, *The Gospel According to John,* Wm. B. Eerdmans Publishing Co., Grand Rapids, 1971, pp. 855–856.

[6] C. F. Keil, *The Books of the Chronicles* in *Biblical Commentary on the Old Testament,* Wm. B. Eerdmans Publishing Co., Grand Rapids, n.d., p. 29.

[7] J. Barton Payne, "1 and 2 Chronicles," Vol. 4, *The Expositor's Bible Commentary,* Zondervan Publishing House, Grand Rapids, 1988, p. 366.

[8] Ibid., p. 439.

[9] Richard D. Patterson and Hermann J. Austel, "1 and 2 Kings," Vol. 4, *The Expositor's Bible Commentary,* Zondervan Publishing House, Grand Rapids, 1988, p. 4.

[10] "Book of Jashar," *The New International Dictionary of the Bible,* Zondervan Publishing House, Grand Rapids, 1987, p. 496.

[11] Ibid.

[12] "Book of the Wars of the Lord," *The Jewish Encyclopedia,* Vol. XII, 1905, p. 468.

[13] Edward C. Pentecost, "Jude," *The Bible Knowledge Commentary: New Testament,* Victor Books, Wheaton, 1983, p. 922.

[14] "Books of Enoch," *The New International Dictionary of the Bible,* Zondervan Publishing House, Grand Rapids, 1987, p. 313.

[15] Pentecost, p. 922.

[16] Israel W. Slotki, *Isaiah,* The Soncino Press Ltd., London, 1949, p. xi.

ENDNOTES

[17] Victor Buksbazen, *The Prophet Isaiah*, The Spearhead Press, Collingswood, N.J., 1971, pp. 42–43.

Chapter 7
[1] Gottlob Schrenk, "graphe, gramma," *Theological Dictionary of the New Testament*, Vol. I, , Wm. B. Eerdmans Publishing Co., Grand Rapids, 1964, p. 765.
[2] Ibid., p. 754.
[3] Eduard Schweizer, "theopneustos," *Theological Dictionary of the New Testament*, Vol. VI, Wm. B. Eerdmans Publishing Co., Grand Rapids, 1968, p. 454.
[4] Schrenk, p. 757.
[5] William F. Arndt and F. Wilbur Gingrich, "epiluo," *A Greek-English Lexicon of the New Testament*, The University of Chicago Press, Chicago, 1957, p. 295.
[6] Arndt and Gingrich, "phero," p. 862.
[7] Konrad Weiss, "phero," *Theological Dictionary of the New Testament*, Vol. IX, Wm. B. Eerdmans Publishing Co., Grand Rapids, 1974, p. 58.
[8] Ibid.
[9] Kenneth L. Barker, "jot," *Wycliffe Bible Encyclopedia*, Vol. 1, Moody Press, Chicago, 1975, p. 962.
[10] Heinrich Schlier, "amen," *Theological Dictionary of the New Testament*, Vol. I, Wm. B. Eerdmans Publishing Co., Grand Rapids, 1964, p. 338.
[11] J. Behm, "anoetos," *Theological Dictionary of the New Testament*, Vol. IV, Wm. B. Eerdmans Publishing Co., Grand Rapids, 1967, pp. 961–962.
[12] Arndt and Gingrich, "luo," p. 485.
[13] Leon Morris, *The Gospel According to John* in *The New International Commentary on the New Testament*, Wm. B. Eerdmans Publishing Co., Grand Rapids, 1971, p. 527.
[14] Ibid., pp. 730–731.
[15] Merrill C. Tenney, "The Gospel of John," Vol. 9, *The Expositor's Bible Commentary*, Zondervan Publishing House, Grand Rapids, 1981, p. 166.
[16] Morris, p. 731.
[17] Arndt and Gingrich, "sugkrino," p. 782.
[18] Eduard Schweizer, "pneumatika," p. 437.

Chapter 8
[1] Abraham Cohen, *Everyman's Talmud*, Schocken Books, New York, 1995, p. 24.
[2] Ibid., p.25.
[3] Gottfried Quell, "kurios," *Theological Dictionary of the New Testament*, Vol. III, Wm. B. Eerdmans Publishing Co., Grand Rapids, 1965, p. 1058.
[4] Eduard Lohse, "huios," *Theological Dictionary of the New Testament*, Vol. VIII, Wm. B. Eerdmans Publishing Co., Grand Rapids, 1972, p. 358.

Chapter 9
[1] D. K. Innes, "Some Notes on Micah," *Evangelical Quarterly*, Vol. 41, No. 3, 1969, p. 170.
[2] Franz Delitzsch, *Biblical Commentary on the Prophecies of Isaiah*, Vol. I, *Biblical Commentaries on*

the Old Testament, Wm. B. Eerdmans Publishing Co., Grand Rapids, 1960, p. 253.

[3] Leon Morris, *The Gospel According to John* in *The New International Commentary on the New Testament*, Wm. B. Eerdmans Publishing Co., Grand Rapids, 1971, p. 73.

[4] Leon Morris, "Hebrews," Vol. 12, *The Expositor's Bible Commentary*, Zondervan Publishing House, Grand Rapids, 1981, p. 64.

[5] Herbert M. Carson, *The Epistles of Paul to the Colossians and Philemon* in *Tyndale New Testament Commentaries*, The Tyndale Press, London, 1960, pp. 42–43.

[6] F. F. Bruce, "Commentary on the Epistle to the Colossians" in *Commentary on the Epistles to the Ephesians and Colossians* in *The New International Commentary on the New Testament*, Wm. B. Eerdmans Publishing Co., Grand Rapids, 1957, p. 194.

[7] Ibid.

[8] William F. Arndt and F. Wilbur Gingrich, "ginomai," *A Greek-English Lexicon of the New Testament*, The University of Chicago Press, Chicago, 1957, p. 157.

Chapter 10

[1] The Aramaic *Targum Jonathan*, quoted by Victor Buksbazen, *The Prophet Isaiah*, The Spearhead Press, Collingswood, N.J., 1971, pp. 163–164.

[2] Franz Delitzsch, *Biblical Commentary on the Prophecies of Isaiah*, Vol. 1, *Biblical Commentaries on the Old Testament*, Wm. B. Eerdmans Publishing Co., Grand Rapids, 1960, p. 253.

[3] Charles Boutflower, *In and Around the Book of Daniel*, Zondervan Publishing House, Grand Rapids, 1963, pp. 54–57.

[4] Leon Morris, *The Gospel According to John* in *The New International Commentary on the New Testament*, Wm. B. Eerdmans Publishing Co., Grand Rapids, 1971, p. 474.

[5] C. K. Barrett, *The Gospel According to St. John*, S.P.C.K., London, 1960, pp. 282–283.

[6] Ibid., p. 283.

[7] Ibid., p. 292.

[8] Morris, p. 474.

[9] Ibid., p. 522.

[10] Eduard Lohse, "*huios*," *Theological Dictionary of the New Testament*, Vol. VIII, Wm. B. Eerdmans Publishing Co., Grand Rapids, 1972, p. 358.

[11] Ethelbert Stauffer, "theos," *Theological Dictionary of the New Testament*, Vol. III, Wm. B. Eerdmans Publishing Co., Grand Rapids, 1965, pp. 81, 83.

[12] H. E. Dana and Julius R. Mantey, *A Manual Grammar of the Greek New Testament*, The Macmillan Company, New York, 1927, pp. 139–140.

[13] Curtis Vaughan, "Colossians," Vol. 11, *The Expositor's Bible Commentary*, Zondervan Publishing House, Grand Rapids, 1978, p. 199.

Chapter 11

[1] J. Dwight Pentecost, *The Words and Works of Jesus Christ*, Zondervan Publishing House, Grand Rapids, 1981, pp. 33–39.

[2] William F. Arndt and F. Wilbur Gingrich, "ginomai," *A Greek-English Lexicon of the New Testament*,

ENDNOTES

The University of Chicago Press, Chicago, 1957, p. 158.

[3] Arndt and Gingrich, "sarx," p. 751.

[4] Wilhelm Michaelis, "skenoo," *Theological Dictionary of the New Testament,* Vol. VII, Wm. B. Eerdmans Publishing Co., Grand Rapids, 1971, p. 386.

[5] Ibid.

[6] Brooke Foss Westcott, *The Epistles of St. John,* Wm. B. Eerdmans Publishing Co., Grand Rapids, 1957, p. 6.

[7] Michaelis, "horao," Vol. V, p. 341.

[8] Westcott, p. 6.

[9] Ibid.

[10] Arndt and Gingrich, "anthropos," p. 67.

[11] H. A. A. Kennedy, "The Epistle to the Philippians," Vol. III, *The Expositor's Greek Testament,* Wm. B. Eerdmans Publishing Co., Grand Rapids, n.d., p. 438.

[12] Johannes Schneider, "homoioma," *Theological Dictionary of the New Testament,* Vol. V, Wm. B. Eerdmans Publishing Co., Grand Rapids, 1967, p. 197.

[13] Schneider, "schema," Vol. VII, p. 956.

[14] Ibid.

[15] F. F. Bruce, "Commentary on the Epistle to the Colossians" in *Commentary on the Epistles to the Ephesians and Colossians* in *The New International Commentary on the New Testament,* Wm. B. Eerdmans Publishing Co., Grand Rapids, 1957, p. 212, footnote 145.

[16] Everett F. Harrison, *Colossians,* Moody Press, Chicago, 1971, pp. 39–40.

[17] Bruce, p. 212.

[18] Rudolf Bultmann and Dieter Luhrmann, "phaneroo," *Theological Dictionary of the New Testament,* Vol. IX, Wm. B. Eerdmans Publishing Co., Grand Rapids, 1974, p. 3.

[19] D. Edmond Hiebert, *First Timothy,* Moody Press, Chicago, 1957, p. 74.

[20] Brooke Foss Westcott, *The Epistle to the Hebrews,* Wm. B. Eerdmans Publishing Co., Grand Rapids, n.d., p. 52.

[21] Arndt and Gingrich, "paraplesios," p. 627.

[22] Westcott, *Hebrews,* p. 52.

[23] F. F. Bruce, *Commentary on the Epistle to the Hebrews* in *The New International Commentary on the New Testament,* Wm. B. Eerdmans Publishing Co., Grand Rapids, 1964, p. 41.

[24] Gerhard Delling, "epilambano," *Theological Dictionary of the New Testament,* Vol. IV, Wm. B. Eerdmans Publishing Co., Grand Rapids, 1967, p. 9.

[25] Friedrich Hauck, "homoioo," *Theological Dictionary of the New Testament,* Vol. V., Wm. B. Eerdmans Publishing Co., Grand Rapids, 1967, p. 563.

[26] Leon Morris, "Hebrews," Vol. 12, *The Expositor's Bible Commentary,* Zondervan Publishing House, Grand Rapids, 1981, p. 29.

[27] Albrecht Oepke, "aner," *Theological Dictionary of the New Testament,* Vol. I, Wm. B. Eerdmans Publishing Co., Grand Rapids, 1964, pp. 361–362.

[28] Arndt and Gingrich, "prospegnumi," p. 725.

[29] Ibid.

[30] Arndt and Gingrich, "anaireo," p. 54.

[31] Arndt and Gingrich, "molops," p. 532.

[32] Arndt and Gingrich, "anthropos," p. 67.

[33] Eduard Lohse, "huios," *Theological Dictionary of the New Testament*, Vol. VIII, Wm. B. Eerdmans Publishing Co., Grand Rapids, 1972, p. 358.

[34] Norval Geldenhuys, *Commentary on the Gospel of Luke* in *The New International Commentary on the New Testament*, Wm. B. Eerdmans Publishing Co., Grand Rapids, 1951, p. 83.

[35] Gustav Stahlin, "prokope," *Theological Dictionary of the New Testament*, Vol. VI, Wm. B. Eerdmans Publishing Co., Grand Rapids, 1968, p. 713.

[36] Schneider, "helikia," Vol. II, p. 942.

[37] Arndt and Gingrich, "embrimaomai," p. 254.

[38] Arndt and Gingrich, "tarasso," p. 813.

[39] Ethelbert Stauffer, "agonia," *Theological Dictionary of the New Testament*, Vol. I, Wm. B. Eerdmans Publishing Co., Grand Rapids, 1964, p. 140.

[40] Arndt and Gingrich, "anthropos," p. 67.

Chapter 12

[1] William F. Arndt and F. Wilbur Gingrich, "hupostasis," *A Greek-English Lexicon of the New Testament*, The University of Chicago Press, Chicago, 1957, p. 854.

[2] Edward J. Young, *The Book of Isaiah*, Vol. 1, Wm. B. Eerdmans Publishing Co., Grand Rapids, 1965, p. 331.

[3] Ibid., p. 337.

[4] Ibid., p. 334.

[5] Gleason L. Archer, Jr., "Daniel," Vol. 7, *The Expositor's Bible Commentary*, Zondervan Publishing House, Grand Rapids, 1985, p. 90.

[6] H. E. Dana and Julius R. Mantey, *A Manual Grammar of the Greek New Testament*, The Macmillan Company, New York, 1927, pp. 139–140.

[7] Arndt and Gingrich, "ginomai," p. 158.

[8] Arndt and Gingrich, "sarx," p. 751.

[9] Wilhelm Michaelis, "skenoo," *Theological Dictionary of the New Testament*, Vol. VII, Wm. B. Eerdmans Publishing Co., Grand Rapids, 1971, p. 386.

[10] Ibid.

[11] Eduard Lohse, "huios," *Theological Dictionary of the New Testament*, Vol. VIII, Wm. B. Eerdmans Publishing Co., Grand Rapids, 1972, p. 358.

[12] John Murray, *The Epistle to the Romans* in *The New International Commentary on the New Testament*, Wm. B. Eerdmans Publishing Co., Grand Rapids, 1968, p. 8.

[13] J. B. Lightfoot, *The Epistle of St. Paul to the Galatians*, Zondervan Publishing House, Grand Rapids, 1957, p. 168.

[14] Herman N. Ridderbos, *The Epistle of Paul to the Churches of Galatia* in *The New International Commentary on the New Testament*, Wm. B. Eerdmans Publishing Co., Grand Rapids, 1953, p. 155.

Chapter 13

[1] William F. Arndt and F. Wilbur Gingrich, "kenoo," *A Greek-English Lexicon of the New Testament*, The

University of Chicago Press, Chicago, 1957, p. 429.

[2] Johannes Schneider, "homoioma," *Theological Dictionary of the New Testament,* Vol. V, Wm. B. Eerdmans Publishing Co., Grand Rapids, 1967, p. 197.

[3] Schneider, "schema," Vol. VII, p. 956.

[4] Ibid.

[5] Curtis Vaughan, "Colossians," Vol. 11, *The Expositor's Bible Commentary,* Zondervan Publishing House, Grand Rapids, 1978, p. 199.

[6] Reinier Schippers, "fullness," *New International Dictionary of New Testament Theology,* Vol. 1, Zondervan Publishing House, Grand Rapids, 1986, p. 740.

[7] Arndt and Gingrich, "morphe," p. 530.

[8] J. Behm, "morphe," *Theological Dictionary of the New Testament,* Vol. IV, Wm. B. Eerdmans Publishing Co., Grand Rapids, 1967, p. 752.

[9] Gustav Stahlin, "isos," *Theological Dictionary of the New Testament,* Vol. III, Wm. B. Eerdmans Publishing Co., Grand Rapids, 1965, p. 353.

[10] Ibid.

[11] Behm, p. 751.

[12] Arndt and Gingrich, "hegeomai," p. 344.

[13] Werner Foerster, "harpagmos," *Theological Dictionary of the New Testament,* Vol. I, Wm. B. Eerdmans Publishing Co., Grand Rapids, 1964, p. 474.

[14] Behm, p. 750.

[15] Ibid., p. 751.

[16] Gerhard Kittel, "hupekoos," *Theological Dictionary of the New Testament,* Vol. I, Wm. B. Eerdmans Publishing Co., Grand Rapids, 1964, p. 225.

[17] Martin Hengel, *Crucifixion,* Fortress Press, Philadelphia, 1977, p. 51.

[18] Georg Bertram, "phroneo," *Theological Dictionary of the New Testament,* Vol. IX, Wm. B. Eerdmans Publishing Co., Grand Rapids, 1974, p. 233.

Chapter 14

[1] Leon Morris, *The Gospel According to John* in *The New International Commentary on the New Testament,* Wm. B. Eerdmans Publishing Co., Grand Rapids, 1971, p. 465.

[2] Merrill C. Tenney, "The Gospel of John," Vol. 9, *The Expositor's Bible Commentary,* Zondervan Publishing House, Grand Rapids, 1981, p. 97.

[3] Gustav Stahlin, "hamartia," *Theological Dictionary of the New Testament,* Vol. I, Wm. B. Eerdmans Publishing Co., Grand Rapids, 1964, p. 295.

[4] David Smith, "The Epistles of John," Vol. V, *The Expositor's Greek Testament,* Wm. B. Eerdmans Publishing Co., Grand Rapids, n.d., pp. 172, 184.

[5] Stahlin.

[6] Friedrich Hauck, "momos," *Theological Dictionary of the New Testament,* Vol. IV, Wm. B. Eerdmans Publishing Co., Grand Rapids, 1967, p. 830.

[7] Ibid., p. 831.

[8] Albrecht Oepke, "aspilos," *Theological Dictionary of the New Testament,* Vol. I, Wm. B. Eerdmans

Publishing Co., Grand Rapids, 1964, p. 502.

[9] Murray J. Harris, "2 Corinthians," Vol. 10, *The Expositor's Bible Commentary,* Zondervan Publishing House, Grand Rapids, 1976, p. 354.

[10] Heinrich Seesemann, "peira," *Theological Dictionary of the New Testament,* Vol. VI, Wm. B. Eerdmans Publishing Co., Grand Rapids, 1968, p. 33.

[11] Leon Morris, "Hebrews," Vol. 12, *The Expositor's Bible Commentary,* Zondervan Publishing House, Grand Rapids, 1981, p. 46.

[12] F. F. Bruce, *Commentary on the Epistle to the Hebrews* in *The New International Commentary on the New Testament,* Wm. B. Eerdmans Publishing Co., Grand Rapids, 1964, p. 86.

[13] Ibid., p. 35.

[14] Tenney, p. 149.

[15] Ibid.

[16] Hauck, "hosios," Vol. V, pp. 490–492.

[17] Walter Grundmann, "akakos," *Theological Dictionary of the New Testament,* Wm. B. Eerdmans Publishing Co., Grand Rapids, 1965, p. 482.

[18] Hauck, "miaino," Vol. IV, p. 647.

[19] Marcus Dods, "The Epistle to the Hebrews," Vol. IV, *The Expositor's Greek Testament,* Wm. B. Eerdmans Publishing Co., Grand Rapids, n.d., p. 318.

[20] Bruce, p. 157.

[21] Hauck, "hosios," p. 492.

[22] William F. Arndt and F. Wilbur Gingrich, "atopos," *A Greek-English Lexicon of the New Testament,* The University of Chicago Press, Chicago, 1957, p. 120.

[23] Gottlob Schrenk, "dikaios," *Theological Dictionary of the New Testament,* Vol. II, Wm. B. Eerdmans Publishing Co., Grand Rapids, 1964, p. 187.

[24] Ibid., p. 189.

[25] Ibid.

[26] Ibid., pp. 188–189.

[27] Ibid, p. 186.

[28] Franz Delitzsch, *Biblical Commentary on the Psalms,* Vol. II, *Biblical Commentaries on the Old Testament,* Wm. B. Eerdmans Publishing Co., Grand Rapids, 1959, pp. 136–137.

[29] H. D. Preuss, "zara," *Theological Dictionary of the Old Testament,* Vol. IV, Wm. B. Eerdmans Publishing Co., Grand Rapids, 1980, pp. 144–145.

[30] Walter C. Kaiser, "zera," *Theological Wordbook of the Old Testament,* Vol. I, Moody Press, Chicago, p. 253.

[31] Arndt and Gingrich, "sperma," p. 769.

[32] Ibid.

[33] Harry A. Hoffner, "bayith," *Theological Dictionary of the Old Testament,* Vol. II, Wm. B. Eerdmans Publishing Co., Grand Rapids, 1975, pp. 113–115.

[34] "Dynasty," *The American College Dictionary,* 1948, p. 377.

[35] Cleon L. Rogers, Jr., "beten," *New International Dictionary of Old Testament Theology & Exegesis,* Vol. 1, Zondervan Publishing House, Grand Rapids, 1997, p. 650.

[36] Ibid., p. 651.

ENDNOTES

37 Ibid.
38 Siegfried Schultz, "sperma," *Theological Dictionary of the New Testament,* Vol. VII, Wm. B. Eerdmans Publishing Co., Grand Rapids, 1971, p. 545.
39 Seesemann, "osphus," Vol. V, p. 497.
40 A. T. Robertson, *A Grammar of the Greek New Testament in the Light of Historical Research,* Broadman Press, Nashville, 1934, p. 576.
41 Ibid., p. 577.
42 Arndt and Gingrich, "ginomai," p. 157.
43 Arndt and Gingrich, "sarx," p. 751.
44 J. A. Motyer, "David," *New International Dictionary of New Testament Theology,* Vol. 1, Zondervan Publishing House, Grand Rapids, 1986, p. 427.
45 Arndt and Gingrich, "genos," p. 155.
46 Robert L. Thomas, *Revelation 8—22,* Moody Press, Chicago, 1995, p. 510.
47 J. Stafford Wright, "son," *New International Dictionary of New Testament Theology,* Vol. 3, Zondervan Publishing House, Grand Rapids, 1986, p. 663.
48 Arndt and Gingrich, "sarx," p. 751.
49 James M. Stifler, *The Epistle to the Romans,* Moody Press, Chicago, 1960, p. 136.
50 John Murray, *The Epistle to the Romans* in *The New International Commentary on the New Testament,* Wm. B. Eerdmans Publishing Co., Grand Rapids, 1968, p. 280.
51 Arndt and Gingrich, "homoioma," p. 570.
52 Murray, p. 280.
53 D. A. Kidd, "peccare," "peccator," *Collins Latin Gem Dictionary,* Collins, London, 1957, p. 601.
54 "Tempt," *The American College Dictionary,* 1948, p. 1247.
55 "Susceptible," *The American College Dictionary,* 1948, p. 1220.
56 Grundmann, "dei," Vol. II, p. 21.
57 Ibid., p. 22.
58 Ibid., p. 23.

Chapter 15
1 "Theocracy," *Webster's New International Dictionary of the English Language,* 2nd ed., 1939, p. 2619.
2 William F. Arndt and F. Wilbur Gingrich, "archon," *A Greek-English Lexicon of the New Testament,* The University of Chicago Press, Chicago, 1957, p. 113.
3 Gottlob Schrenk, "boulomai," *Theological Dictionary of the New Testament,* Vol. I, Wm. B. Eerdmans Publishing Co., Grand Rapids, 1964, p. 632, text and footnote 53.
4 Victor P. Hamilton, "shup," *Theological Wordbook of the Old Testament,* Vol. II, Moody Press, Chicago, 1980, p. 912.

Chapter 16
1 William F. Arndt and F. Wilbur Gingrich, "thronos," *A Greek-English Lexicon of the New Testament,* The University of Chicago Press, Chicago, 1957, p. 365.
2 Wilhelm Michaelis, "kratos," *Theological Dictionary of the New Testament,* Vol. III, Wm. B.

Eerdmans Publishing Co., Grand Rapids, 1965, pp. 907–908.

[3] Walter Grundmann, "dunamis," *Theological Dictionary of the New Testament,* Vol. II, Wm. B. Eerdmans Publishing Co., Grand Rapids, 1964, p. 295.

[4] Ibid., pp. 292, 306.

[5] Alfred Jenour, *Rational Apocalypticum,* Vol. I, Thomas Hatchard, London, 1852, p. 202.

[6] Richard D. Patterson, "seper," *Theological Wordbook of the Old Testament,* Vol. II, Moody Press, Chicago, 1980, p. 633.

[7] Gottfried Fitzer, "sphragis," *Theological Dictionary of the New Testament,* Vol. VII, Wm. B. Eerdmans Publishing Co., Grand Rapids, 1971, p. 940.

Chapter 17

[1] Robert L. Thomas, *Revelation 8–22,* Moody Press, Chicago, 1995, p. 106.

Chapter 19

[1] Friedrich Bushel, "palingenesia," *Theological Dictionary of the New Testament,* Vol. 1, Wm. B. Eerdmans Publishing Co., Grand Rapids, 1964, p. 686.

[2] William F. Arndt and F. Wilbur Gingrich, "palin," *A Greek-English Lexicon of the New Testament,* The University of Chicago Press, Chicago, 1957, p. 611.

[3] Ibid.

[4] Arndt and Gingrich, "hopos," p. 580.

[5] Arndt and Gingrich, "anapsuxis," p. 63.

[6] Albrecht Oepke, "apokatastasis," *Theological Dictionary of the New Testament,* Vol. 1, Wm. B. Eerdmans Publishing Co., Grand Rapids, 1964, p. 391.

[7] Ibid., p. 389.

[8] Ibid., p. 391.

[9] F. F. Bruce, *Commentary on the Book of Acts* in *The New International Commentary on the New Testament,* Wm. B. Eerdmans Publishing Co., Grand Rapids, 1954, p. 91, footnote 36.

[10] Arndt and Gingrich, "mataiotes," p. 496.

[11] Arndt and Gingrich, "phthora," p. 865.

[12] Arndt and Gingrich, "apekdechomai," p. 82.

[13] Everett F. Harrison, "Romans," Vol. 10, *The Expositor's Bible Commentary,* Zondervan Publishing House, Grand Rapids, 1976, p. 94.

[14] William Sanday and Arthur C. Headlam, *A Critical and Exegetical Commentary on the Epistle to the Romans* in *The International Critical Commentary,* T. & T. Clark, Edinburgh, 1958, p. 206.

[15] Ibid., p. 207.

[16] Ibid.

[17] John Murray, *The Epistle to the Romans* in *The New International Commentary on the New Testament,* Wm. B. Eerdmans Publishing Co., Grand Rapids, 1965, p. 302, footnote 26.

Chapter 21

[1] William F. Arndt and F. Wilbur Gingrich, "eggizo," *A Greek-English Lexicon of the New Testament,* The

ENDNOTES

University of Chicago Press, Chicago, 1957, p. 212.

[2] Gerhard Delling, "kairos," *Theological Dictionary of the New Testament,* Vol. III, Wm. B. Eerdmans Publishing Co., Grand Rapids, 1965, p. 459.

[3] Ibid.

[4] Rudolf Bultmann, "ginosko," *Theological Dictionary of the New Testament,* Vol. I, Wm. B. Eerdmans Publishing Co., Grand Rapids, 1964, pp. 704–705.

GENERAL INDEX

GENERAL INDEX

SCRIPTURE INDEX

NOTE: *Italic* numbers in this Index refer to pages on which the verses listed are cited.